Mental Health
from Diagnosis to Delivery

Also from the Boys Town Press

Teaching Social Skills to Youth

Basic Social Skills for Youth

Tools for Teaching Social Skills in School

More Tools for Teaching Social Skills in School

Building Resiliency in Youth: A Trauma-Informed Guide
   for Working with Youth in School

Building Resiliency in Children Activity Guide

Building Resiliency in Teens Workbook

No Room for Bullies

Working with Aggressive Youth

Common Sense Parenting®

Common Sense Parenting of Toddlers and Preschoolers

Well-Managed Schools

Take Two: Skill-Building Skits You Have Time to Do!

13 & Counting: Be the Difference

13 & Counting: Rescue Me?

13 & Counting: Does a Hamburger Have to Be Round?

Everyone's Talking: Stories to Engage Middle Schoolers

Positive Alternatives to Suspension

For Adolescents

Boundaries: A Guide for Teens

A Good Friend

Middle School Misfits

He's Not Just Teasing

Am I Weird?

I Lost My BFF

The Good, the Bad, and the Backstory

Why Is He Spreading Rumors about Me?

My Anxiety Is Messing Things Up

Why Is Drama Always Following Me?

Butterflies in Me: An anthology bringing awareness to mental health

For a free Boys Town Press catalog, call 1-800-282-6657
Visit our website at BoysTownPress.org

Boys Town National Hotline®
1-800-448-3000
A crisis, resource, and referral number for kids and parents

Boys Town, Nebraska

Mental Health

from Diagnosis to Delivery

How to Incorporate Effective
Social Skills Teaching into **Treatment Plans**

KAT MCGRADY, EdD, LCPC, NCC

CONTRIBUTING AUTHORS
Jennifer Resetar Volz, PhD and Tara Snyder, PsyD

Mental Health from Diagnosis to Delivery

Published by Boys Town Press
Boys Town, NE 68010
Copyright © 2022 by Father Flanagan's Boys' Home

ISBN: 978-1-944882-98-3

Boys Town Press is the publishing division of Boys Town, a national organization serving children and families.

Publisher's Cataloging in Publication

Names: McGrady, Kat, author.

Title: Mental health from diagnosis to delivery : how to incorporate effective social skills teaching into treatment plans / Kat McGrady.

Description: Boys Town, NE : Boys Town Press, [2022] | Includes index.

Identifiers: ISBN: 978-1-944882-98-3

Subjects: LCSH: Mental health counseling. | Children--Counseling of. | Teenagers--Counseling of. | Child psychotherapy. | Adolescent psychotherapy. | Social skills in children--Study and teaching. | Social interaction in children--Study and teaching. | Interpersonal relations in children-- Study and teaching. | Social learning--Study and teaching. | Socialization--Study and teaching. | Emotional maturity--Study and teaching. | Social work with children. | Social work with teenagers. | Resilience (Personality trait) in adolescence--Study and teaching. | Resilience (Personality trait) in children--Study and teaching. | BISAC: EDUCATION / Counseling / Crisis Management. | EDUCATION / Special Education / Behavioral, Emotional & Social Disabilities. | PSYCHOLOGY / Psychotherapy / Child & Adolescent. | PSYCHOLOGY / Psychotherapy / Counseling. | PSYCHOLOGY / Psychopathology / Attention-Deficit Disorder (ADD-ADHD) | PSYCHOLOGY / Psychopathology / Anxieties & Phobias. | PSYCHOLOGY / Psychopathology / Autism Spectrum Disorders. | PSYCHOLOGY / Psychopathology / Depression.

Classification: LCC: RC480.5 .M34 2022 | DDC: 616.89/14--dc23

15 14 13 12 11 10 9 8 7 6 5 4 3 2 1

⟩⟩⟩ *Table of Contents*

Introduction

irresponsible **angry**
follower clown high
unpredictable defiant scared
rude low unruly paranoid
energetic careless pain *lazy* quiet
selfish squirmy joker
weird irritating
liar troublemaker loud
irritated spoiled loner **bully**
pest unmotivated
zombie obsessive numb busy
emotional daredevil

"They are just so angry all the time. It's like a constant power struggle. The only things that come out of their mouths are name-calling, defiance, or yelling."

"That child is just too emotional. They need to quit being so spoiled and deal with the fact that they can't always get what they want."

"They always sit by themselves and refuse to take part in the fun activities I have planned. Do they even want friends or to have fun?!"

"The kid is a tornado. Nonstop and always charged. I just wish they would stop for one minute and focus. Ugh!"

"They are just so weird. Obsessing over things that don't matter, unable to stop and think about something else; it's like they are in their own world."

"It's like I'm talking to a robot. No emotion, no remorse, no shame or empathy. Not even a smile when we are having a good day!"

We have heard the comments. The labels. The tales and exhausted utterances of frustrated and defeated teachers, caregivers, and treatment providers doing their best to support children and adolescents who seem to be categorically impenetrable and beyond reach. The "go-to" strategies and approaches seem ineffective. Added, extensive behavioral or academic procedures seem futile. The youth becomes an enigma to those supporting them. In these instances, it is more likely than not that there is an underlying mental health condition at play.

The concept of child and adolescent mental health disorders is relatively new and misunderstood. Previously stigmatized, doubted, and ignored by many, the increase in and study of child and adolescent mental health disorders has raised awareness and lessened the stigma. Research and understanding of the impact of these disorders is ongoing and ever-changing as our youth face previously unseen social and cultural challenges, immediate and exhaustive access to worldly distressing events via technology and social media, and various other biological, psychological, social, and environmental factors.

The Centers for Disease Control and Prevention (CDC) describes childhood mental health disorders as "serious changes in the ways children typically learn, behave, or handle their emotions." According to the National Alliance on Mental Illness (NAMI), half of all mental illness begins by age 14. It is estimated that nearly one in six children and adolescents have a diagnosable mental health disorder in the United States; yet, a 2016 study conducted by JAMA (Journal of the American Medical Association) Pediatrics found that nearly half of these youth are left untreated.

Oftentimes, these conditions go overlooked, undiagnosed, or misdiagnosed (Whitney & Peterson, 2019).

The cause of these phenomena can stem from a number of factors, including:

- Similar criteria and characteristics between various mental health conditions

- Unreliable observations or testing conditions

- Basing impressions on stereotypical identifiers that may not be accurate or comprehensive

- Making assumptions of unevaluated and undiagnosed children and lumping them into a universally known condition

- A child's ability to "hide," compensate for, or silence their conditions

This can lead to misalignment and mismanagement of behavioral, academic, and social-emotional goals and accommodations. Such misalignment then impacts caregiver and treatment provider education and appreciation of proper responses, tools, and strategies to best support the needs of children and adolescents. Results of improper support can span social, emotional, academic, and behavioral spectrums. Self-image, self-confidence, and overall self-acceptance can waiver, as well.

The Diagnostic and Statistical Manual of Mental Disorders (5th ed.; DSM–5; American Psychiatric Association, 2013) is one of the world's standard tools for evaluating and diagnosing mental health disorders in children, adolescents, and adults. Progress in classifying and identifying mental health disorders has led to improved instruction and training for treatment providers that are more intensely focused on how to effectively treat youth with specific mental health disorders. This, in turn, has led to more appropriate and accurate treatment for youth.

While a correct diagnosis and treatment are imperative, it is equally important for caregivers, treatment providers, and the child in question to have a full understanding of what the diagnosis means. The more caregivers and providers understand the diagnosis in both general and individualized terms, the more they can educate the child about their condition. With greater understanding, the child may avoid feelings of shame, inferiority, and self-judgment. This knowledge also can help maximize the skills and strategies taught, create data-driven goals, establish proper accommodations, and provide precise ongoing support.

Helping caregivers and treatment providers further improve the care they provide youth with mental health disorders is the goal of this book. Through years of experience working with thousands of children and adolescents with behavioral and mental disorders, Boys Town's research has proven that social skill instruction – teaching youth alternative positive behaviors they can use to replace current inappropriate behavior – is extremely effective in helping youth overcome their problems. In many situations, a lack of certain social skills can contribute to, and often exacerbate, an existing mental health disorder. A lack of social skills may lead to new or heightened issues surrounding relationships, mental health, self-confidence, emotional regulation, and academics, and can also lead to reckless and maladaptive coping behaviors. On the other hand, purposeful social skills training can increase overall well-being and benefit major life domains, including:

- **Academics** – help youth set and manage goals, problem-solve, listen actively, communicate needs, follow directions, be flexible and adaptable to change, etc.

- **Relationships** – help youth with communication, cooperation and teamwork, assertiveness, maintaining conversations, active listening, conflict resolution, empathy, social cue recognition, etc.

- **Sense of Self** – help youth with confidence, awareness of self and the environment, the ability to express self and regulate emotions, self-identity, self-control, lessening stress, increasing overall happiness and quality of life, etc.

By showing how this social skill instruction approach can be applied to the treatment of DSM-5 disorders, this book serves as a valuable guide in helping treatment providers effectively and successfully treat youth in their care. (Treatment providers can include youth care workers, group home caregivers, consultants, foster parents, shelter workers and administrators, family interventionists, staff working in psychiatric settings, teachers, school counselors, therapists, social workers, psychiatrists, physicians, psychologists, clinicians, and other health and mental health professionals.)

What's in This Book

There are six parts to this book. A history of the DSM-5 is outlined in the first chapter, along with an introduction to the importance of other mental health disorder assessment and evaluation tools. Additional considerations such as (1) self-diagnosis, (2) how to distinguish between mental health, behavioral health, and learning disabilities, and (3) steps for parents to take if they suspect a disorder, are included. A discussion of individualized treatment planning regarding DSM-5 mental health disorder diagnoses and social skill instruction follows in the second chapter.

The third chapter builds on the information in chapters 1 and 2 by adding additional keys to the successful creation of an initial treatment plan. The keys include data collection, communication, and a collaborative team effort. The fourth chapter highlights the Boys Town Model®, the Boys Town Social Skills Curriculum, the concept of social skill instruction, and the importance and effectiveness of such teaching in the treatment of mental health disorders.

Chapter 5 offers a series of charts containing DSM-5 diagnoses that are common for children and adolescents, and the various social skills that caregivers and treatment providers might target as part of a treatment plan for each disorder. These charts don't include all DSM-5 disorders, but those that are likely to have associated social skills deficits that might be targeted in treatment. The various disorders and charts are listed in the order they appear in the DSM-5.

Examples of treatment plans are included in the final chapter. These examples demonstrate how social skills can be integrated into a youth's overall treatment plan for particular DSM-5 diagnoses across different settings – home and school, residential group home, and psychiatric facility – and levels of care. Additionally, Chapter 6 includes key terms to know in treatment planning, key dates and time frames as mandated by state and national legislation, and next steps to consider if the treatment plan is insufficient or is not being followed as agreed upon by all stakeholders.

It is important to note that only qualified professionals who have had the proper schooling, clinical training, and experience should use the DSM-5 to evaluate and diagnose youth who may have a mental health disorder. This book is intended only as a guide for how to integrate social skills training into treatment planning and should not be used to make diagnoses. Youth will see a therapist, psychologist, or psychiatrist for assessment and diagnostic purposes. An accurate DSM-5 diagnosis enables caregivers and treatment providers across the entire spectrum of settings – home, schools, shelters, foster care, residential treatment programs, psychiatric treatment settings, etc. – to develop better, more effective treatment plans.

We hope you find this book useful in your work with children and adolescents. All youth must learn social skills in order to find success in their lives. Teaching these social skills as part of treatment for a mental health disorder can truly enhance a youth's progress and help them to overcome problems.

Chapter 1

Psychological Assessment and the DSM-5

The initial impetus for developing a classification of mental health disorders was the collection of statistical information for the U.S. Census back in 1840. At that time, there was one crude category for such disorders – "idiocy/insanity." By the 1880 census, there were seven categories of mental illnesses. This gathering of statistical information on mental health disorders continued until 1952. That's when the first edition of the *Diagnostic and Statistical Manual of Mental Disorders* (or DSM-I) was published by the American Psychiatric Association (APA). This manual contained a glossary of descriptions of the diagnostic categories and was the first official manual of mental health disorders designed for clinical use. Shortly thereafter, the DSM-II, which contained a new round of diagnostic revisions, was published. The DSM-III followed in 1980. It introduced a number of important methodological innovations and a descriptive approach that attempted to be neutral with respect to the theories of etiology. In 1987, the APA published the DSM-III-R, which contained revisions and corrections for inconsistencies and instances where criteria were not entirely clear in the DSM-III (American Psychiatric Association, 1994).

The DSM-IV, published in 1994, came about due to the substantial increase in research that was generated by the DSM-III and DSM-III-R. By that time, research regarding diagnoses was available in the empirical literature or other data sets. The DSM-IV content was based on "...historical tradition (as embodied in the DSM-III and DSM-III-R), evidence from reviews of the literature, analyses of unpublished data sets, results of field trials, and consensus of the field" (American Psychiatric Association, 2000, p. xxvii). The DSM-IV included 340 mental health disorders, nearly 120 more than the DSM III-R. In 2000, the DSM-IV-TR was released in order to address necessary text revisions. There were no major changes to diagnostic criteria, and no diagnoses were added or removed; the revisions were mainly to correct errors and provide updates.

The DSM-5

2013 saw the biggest changes to the DSM in years. According to the APA, these changes served to ensure more consistent and accurate diagnoses and to assist researchers in studying the relationship between various diagnoses.

One of the most obvious and easily noticeable changes was the shift of edition identification from Roman numerals to standard Arabic. This allows for ease of tracking of future editions. The next fundamental change was the evolution of the categorical blueprint from the previous multiaxial system to a simplified and more succinct system. The Global Assessment of Functioning (GAF score) was also removed due to its "lack of conceptual clarity and questionable psychometric measures" (American Psychological Association, 2013). Taking its place is now precisely categorized disorders listed along with related disorders, which allows for clarity and ease of retrieval. Additionally, a number of formal diagnoses were added while others were removed. Some diagnoses were not added or removed, but rather were lifted from their previous sections and placed into categories that better align with the most current research.

Further, the DSM-5 was framed to harmonize with the World Health Organization's International Classification of Diseases, 11th Edition (ICD-11), which was revised around the same time as the DSM revision. According to the APA, this purposeful alignment took place in order to: (a) minimize discrepancies and ambivalence between the two diagnostic tools, (b) reduce research complications associated with having to reconcile two mental health classifications when attempting to replicate scientific results, (c) avoid obstacles to the design of clinical trials and the collection of national health statistics, and (d) lessen the impediments of global applicability of research findings by international regulatory agencies (American Psychiatric Association, 2013).

In an effort to increase awareness of emerging models and measures, the DSM-5 placed assessment measures and guidance on cultural formulation, alternative diagnostic models, and conditions for further study in Section III of the manual. Previous editions arranged this content in the appendices, as explained by the APA.

The DSM-5 takes into account the importance of understanding diversity when diagnosing and treating mental health disorders. According to the APA, the DSM-5 addresses cross-cultural variations in manifestation, presentation, and in clinical work. By addressing the three concepts of cultural syndrome, cultural idiom of distress, and cultural explanation or perceived cause, the DSM-5 offers greater utility for clinicians working with diverse populations (American Psychiatric Association, 2013). Sex and gender differences are taken to account in this edition of the DSM, as it includes multi-tiered information on sex and gender differences, both biological and individual self-representation. What's more, this latest edition contains an interview tool that can be used to facilitate person-centered assessments in order to take the individual into account when determining a diagnosis and treatment plan.

Childhood and Adolescent Disorders in the Newest Edition of the DSM

Changes made in the newest edition of the DSM include the removal of disorders that are usually "first diagnosed in infancy, childhood, or adolescence" and the addition of childhood disorders such as social communication disorder and disruptive mood dysregulation disorder. Additionally, the DSM-5 is organized to align with the human lifespan rather than by axis, as research suggests that age and development is integral in understanding mental disorders.

Criticisms of the DSM-5

As the official diagnostic tool used predominantly in the United States, the DSM-5 naturally has been scrutinized by a number of experts in the field. In an effort to illuminate strengths, areas of improvement, and possible next steps in future revisions, critics of the DSM-5 describe components that they feel are inadequate.

Perhaps the most glaring and popular criticism of the DSM-5 is that of the questionable quality of scientific reliability and validity, as the tool relies heavily on subjective elements as opposed to concrete and objective measures (Guterman, 2017; Young, 2013). In fact, the National Institute of Mental Health (NIMH) has backed away from supporting the DSM for the purposes of research (although the institution still endorses the tool for clinical use) due to its lack of scientific validity. Instead, the NIMH has created the Research Domain Criteria framework (RDoC) which is intended to be used in mental health research. Others have cited the lack of disclosure and documentation when outlining the revised tool's creation as a means to question its overall integrity (Wakefield, 2016). Another criticism involves the pathologization of the DSM-5 and how this could possibly lead to a reliance on stereotypes and the seeking of diagnosis in such a way that it may lead to overdiagnosis. Medicinization and politics may also be at play, according to some critics. Their argument includes the heavy reliance on the pharmacological world and insurance industry in the creation of the

DSM-5, as well as the fact that powerful institutions have deemed the DSM a major player in the diagnostic game, which could indicate politics are at play. A final argument revolves around the lack of ability to guide treatment goals and plans due to the absence of objective measures.

Regardless of the criticisms and possible shortcomings, most agree that the DSM-5 is a useful diagnostic tool. Just as medical doctors face new and/or morphing conditions, those in the mental health field must contend with ever-changing symptoms, new conditions, must continuously research and learn, and must understand how biological, psychological, social, and environmental factors impact mental health. While the DSM is subject to dispute, it is an ever-evolving tool that continuously refines itself to remain a practical, effective, and relevant guide in the mental health field.

DSM-5 and Diagnostic Assessment

The DSM-5 is generally one of the first evaluation tools utilized by trained and knowledgeable mental health professionals to accurately diagnose mental health disorders. Other information can come from youth interviews, parent/guardian interviews, teacher interviews, medical records, educational records, educational assessments, psychological assessments, behavioral observations, and other measures. The use of these methods allows mental health professionals to gather more detailed information about a youth's unique areas of need, and possible root causes behind deficits, thus helping to strengthen the accuracy of the evaluation and diagnostic process.

Another important diagnostic tool used in conjunction with the DSM-5 is the World Health Organization's International Statistical Classification of Diseases and Related Health Problems (ICD-11). This official world classification system is used by all health practitioners and includes a substantial section dedicated solely to mental health disorders. The ICD-11 is a bit more comprehensive than the DSM-5, yet it does not provide the same level of clear diagnostic criteria as the DSM-5. While this has led some to question the accuracy of the ICD-11, others appreciate the broader scale of coding and the discretion this provides clinicians in determining a diagnosis.

Psychological assessments are often used by mental health professionals when considering diagnosis. These assessments include a range of techniques such as report forms, scales, observational data, clinical interviews, or comprehensive data collection tools (US Department of Health and Human Services, 2016). The table below describes commonly used psychological assessments:

	Comprehensive		
	Achenbach System for Empirically Based Assessment (ASEBA)	**Behavior Assessment System for Children, Third Edition (BASC-3)**	**Conners' Comprehensive Behavior Rating Scales (CBRS)**
Measured	Competencies, strengths, adaptive functioning, social problems, emotional problems, behavioral problems	Behavior and self-perception	Behavior, emotional, and academic disorders
Instruments	Child Behavior Checklist (CBCL), Caregiver-Teacher Report Form (C-TRF or TRF), Youth Self Report (YSR), Multicultural Supplements, Semistructured Clinical Interview for Children and Adolescents (SCICA), Brief Problem Monitor (BPM)	Parent Rating Scales (PRS), Teacher Rating Scales (TRS), Student Observation System (SOS), Structured Developmental History (SDH), Self-Report of Personality (SRP), Parent Relationship Questionnaire (PRQ)	Parent Response Booklet (P), Teacher Response Booklet (T), and Self-Report Response Booklet (SR)
Source	https://aseba.org/aseba-overview/	https://www.pearsonassessments.com/store/usassessments/en/Store/Professional-Assessments/Behavior/Comprehensive/Behavior-Assessment-System-for-Children-%7C-Third-Edition-/p/100001402.html?tab=product-details	https://www.wpspublish.com/conners-cbrs-conners-comprehensive-behavior-rating-scales
Additional Information	Achenbach & Rescorla, 2001	Reynolds & Kamphaus, 2015	Conners, 2008

	Clinical Interview-Based		
	Child and Adolescent Psychiatric Assessment (CAPA)	**Preschool Age Psychiatric Assessment (PAPA)**	**Diagnostic Interview Schedule for Children (DISC-5)**
Measured	Mental health disorders	Mental health disorders	Mental health disorders
Instruments	Parent interview, Child interview	Parent interview	Parent interview, Child interview
Source	https://devepi.duhs.duke.edu/measures/the-child-and-adolescent-psychiatric-assessment-capa/	https://devepi.duhs.duke.edu/measures/the-preschool-age-psychiatric-assessment-papa/	https://pubmed.ncbi.nlm.nih.gov/10638065/
Additional Information	Angold, Prendergast, Cox, Harrington, Simonoff, & Rutter, 1995	Egger & Angold, 2004	Shaffer et al., 2000

These assessment tools produce a variety of information about a youth's perceived behavioral, emotional, and social functioning. The method employed will depend on a youth's age, available informants, and the specific information that is desired. Scores on these assessments can help to indicate frequency, severity, and extent of symptoms when compared to a baseline score determined by youth of similar demographics. This information also can be helpful when planning and evaluating treatment plans for particular youth, as they provide clarity on social, emotional, and psychological areas of improvement, can determine factors leading to academic and/or behavioral concerns, and often include recommendations for IEP goals and supports.

Educational assessments also are used by mental health professionals and school personnel to provide information about a youth's cognitive ability or achievement. These scores are important to consider when developing treatment plans. For example, if a youth's verbal ability is significantly below average, a treatment strategy that relies heavily on language would not be appropriate for that youth.

Cognitive ability provides information about an individual's capabilities in a variety of areas (verbal comprehension, perceptual reasoning, processing speed, working memory, etc.) and is often termed an individual's intelligence quotient or "IQ." There are numerous tests that measure IQ; each differs in the appropriate age range for testing and the specific domains of intelligence that are considered. Some common examples include:

- Wechsler Preschool and Primary Scale of Intelligence, Fourth Edition (WPPSI-IV) (Wechsler, 2012)

- Wechsler Intelligence Scale for Children, Fifth Edition (WISC-V) (Wechsler, 2014)

- Wechsler Adult Intelligence Scale, Fourth Edition (WAIS-IV) (Wechsler, 2008)

- Wechsler Abbreviated Scale of Intelligence, Second Edition (WASI-II) (Wechsler, 2011)

- Stanford-Binet Intelligence Scale, Fifth Edition (SB5) (Roid, 2003)

- The Woodcock-Johnson IV Tests of Cognitive Abilities, Fourth Edition (WJ-IV COG; Schrank, McGrew, & Mather, 2014)

Achievement is the level at which an individual is currently performing in a given academic area (reading, mathematics, written language, oral language, etc.). Achievement scores are used to determine whether an individual meets criteria for a learning disability. Generally, a large discrepancy between one's ability and one's achievement indicates that a learning disability may be present, since the individual is not achieving at the level that would be expected.

Examples of achievement measures include:

- Wechsler Individual Achievement Test, Fourth Edition (WIAT-4) (Wechsler, 2020)

- Woodcock Johnson IV Tests of Achievement (WJ-IV) (Woodcock, McGrew, & Mather, 2014)

- The Woodcock-Johnson IV Tests of Cognitive Abilities, Fourth Edition (WJ-IV COG; Schrank, McGrew, & Mather, 2014)

- Wide Range Achievement Test, Fifth Edition (WRAT-5) (Wilkinson & Robertson, 2017)

Many types of assessment methods can be used to help mental health professionals arrive at an appropriate diagnosis. These methods also can be helpful when developing treatment plans and evaluating the effectiveness of interventions. The assessment measures highlighted earlier are commonly used in determining the breadth and scope of proficiencies and deficiencies, however, they represent a mere portion of numerous valid and reliable assessments available for professional use.

Important Diagnosis Considerations: Self-Diagnosis

While the DSM-5 is easily accessible, it is important to note that this, as with any other diagnostic tool, is only to be used by trained professionals who are qualified to assess, diagnose, and treat mental illness. Moreover, self-diagnosis, even when based on scales and measurements online or in other mediums, can be dangerously misleading. It is vital that well-established and appropriate professional guidance and treatment is provided when a suspected diagnosis is present.

Self-Diagnosis in Pre-Teens and Teens

Self-diagnosis and self-labeling are becoming an increasing phenomenon in the pre-teen and teen age range. Reasons for this can include:

- Social media normalization and/or social connection in general

- A sense of uniqueness/attention-seeking

- Curiosity

- Excusability of certain behaviors

- Desire to explore medications

- Lack of education and awareness of mental health conditions

This can negatively impact not only the youth in question but those around them as well. Self-diagnosis could lead to inadvertent exaggeration of conditions, self-stigmatizing, and negative impacts on overall well-being (Moses, 2009). A self-diagnosis could impact the way that others treat the youth and could be detrimental to any peers or members in their community who actually have the condition in question.

If you support and/or care for a child or teen who has self-diagnosed, consider these tips when addressing the issue:

- Talk to them. Try to understand where they are coming from. What makes them feel like they have this condition?

- What are the potential positives of being diagnosed with this condition?

- Do they have peers who have the same condition or who have explored the idea of possibly having this condition?

- What are some alternatives aside from this condition that could account for their feelings, thoughts, and actions?

- Educate them. Research the condition using multiple sources, encourage them to ask questions, and work with them to increase their understanding.

- Explore appropriate coping strategies with them.

- Encourage them to partake in activities that increase self-esteem, confidence, and sense of self.

- Talk to a professional with them.

Cultural Elements

Awareness and appreciation of diversity in diagnosis and treatment is a key advancement of the DSM-5. Experts agree that culture influences all aspects of mental health and the effectiveness of treatment. In the *2000 Report of the Surgeon General's Conference of Children's Mental Health: A National Action Agenda*, the US Department of Health and Human Services (DHHS), the US Department of Education, and the US Department of Justice address the importance of cultural awareness in diagnosis and treatment of youth with mental health disorders. In fact, one of their goals for improvement of children's mental health care included the "[elimination of] racial/ethnic and socioeconomic disparities in access to mental healthcare services" (DHHS, 2000; Whitney & Peterson, 2019). Action steps to reach this goal included measures to increase the following:

- accessibility of culturally competent services

- targeted research-driven and evidence-based services

- resource capacity within schools

- school, community, and family stakeholder connection and alignment in treatment and services provided

- family engagement in awareness, prevention, and intervention

- research on diagnosis, treatment, prevention, and focused services within diverse populations

While progress has been made in research, professional training, and in overall strides to reach this goal, there are still gaps and areas for improvement. Therefore, it is important to take into consideration the whole child when diagnosing and treating mental health disorders. Some areas to consider include:

- background and history

- family system, values, and beliefs

- stigma around diagnosis and/or treatment

- coping styles and patterns of treatment-seeking

- how the youth identifies and relates to the world around them

- perceptions and communication of underlying conditions

- historical impact (biases, discrimination, etc.)

- community and immediate environment

- social and support systems

- other possible barriers (from treatment providers and the individual being treated) and how to mitigate them.

Parents and Caregivers: When Seeking Professional Guidance in a Possible Diagnosis

Mental Health vs. Behavioral Health vs. Learning Disability: What's the Difference?

At times, mental health conditions can be confused with behavioral disorders or with learning disabilities. These conditions are often used interchangeably, however, there are some distinctions that may be important to note when determining a course of action.

Mental health refers to psychological, biological, and behavioral factors and their impact on overall wellness. It examines thought processes, ability to cope with daily life stressors, and actions. Behavioral health deals more with actions, habits, responses to the environment, and how these elements impact well-being.

The National Association of Special Education Teachers states that learning disabilities affect the brain's ability to receive, process, store, and respond to information. The Mental Health Foundation explains that learning disabilities are lifelong and are typically diagnosed in early childhood. While they cannot be "treated" in the same sense of mental health and behavioral disorders, support can be received to decrease boundaries and increase productivity and overall happiness.

While these distinctions may help guide plans of action, it is important to note that these conditions can occur comorbidly. Proper diagnosis and distinction between conditions, as well as a team of specialized supports, may be needed in this case.

What to Do if You Suspect a Disorder

If you suspect the possibility of a mental health condition, behavioral health condition, or learning disability, there are a number of steps you can take. Initial steps include:

- Talk to the school. Make them aware of your concerns, ask what they have observed, and brainstorm possibilities for data collection, information gathering, and next steps.

- Request that the school psychologist, resource team, or equivalent provide input. While they are unable to diagnose a student, they can determine if a child or adolescent displays tendencies toward a mental health disorder or learning disability. Results could be used to determine eligibility for a treatment plan.

- Talk to other caregivers and adults in your child's life (coach, tutor, camp counselors, after-school group leaders, etc.) to better understand what they have observed.

- Talk to your child's pediatrician. Explain what you have observed and listen to their thoughts. They may provide you with scales to complete, referrals for further guidance, or actionable steps to take in the short-term.

- Talk to a mental health professional. An assessment or screening by a qualified professional will provide a strong foundational understanding of what is going on.

- Inquire about possible tests that would help to rule out or pinpoint possibilities. Lab tests, physical exams, evaluation of personal history, and mental health screenings can help paint a picture. Psychological tests and neuropsychological evaluations can add even more color to this picture.

- Explore resources related to the rights of youth and education, such as the Individuals with Disabilities Education Act (IDEA), section 504 of the Rehabilitation Act, WrightsLaw, the National Alliance on Mental Illness school page, or request information from your school on resources that they have available.

Next Steps in Seeking School Support

Once a diagnosis has been determined, it is important that the school becomes aware so that they can provide the proper support via a treatment plan. The best approach would be sending an email to school administration, the school counselor (or resource counselor), at least one member of the school resource/special education team, your child's homeroom teacher, and the school nurse (if a health plan should be considered) clearly stating the diagnosis (attach all testing and relevant documents if possible) and your formal written request for a meeting to determine next steps.

If a diagnosis has not been made by an outside professional, but you strongly suspect a disability, you may still send a formal written request for an evaluation meeting. In this communication, however, you will request that a full evaluation or assessment be made in all areas of suspected disabilities (there are 14 IEP-eligible categories that fall under the IDEA Act), a detailed description of concerns and how specific needs are not being met by the school, consent for the school to perform these evaluations, and any relevant information from the pediatrician, therapist, and other professional outside supports. The school may evaluate skills such as functional, adaptive, OT/PT, speech, social-emotional, academic, and/or other focused areas where a diagnosis may be present.

The school will then send you a date to meet with the Educational Management Team (EMT). Before the meeting, it may be helpful to:

- Request a blank copy of the IEP/504 form to prepare yourself for the questions and format.

- Gather all testing results, notes, and observations (formal and informal, from all stakeholders), and other relevant documents (health history and educational history if the child/adolescent attended other schools).

- Familiarize yourself with your rights as a parent with a child who has a treatment plan (the school typically has this available for you upon request).

- Write a list of your child's strengths, weaknesses, and goals that you would like to see written in (consider academic, social, emotional, and behavioral goals).

- Write any questions you may have (this may be a list that you build on in the days leading up to the meeting) to ensure you do not forget to ask during the meeting.

- Connect with parents who have a child with a treatment plan.

- Consider bringing outside supports (let the school know if you are doing so, though) such as educational consultants/advocates, lawyers, or private therapists or other outside supports who have been working with your child.

- Consider writing and printing multiple copies of a "snapshot" describing your child. You could include items such as: name, age, homeroom teacher, hobbies/interest, relevant educational and medical history, developmental milestones, major life experiences that may have impacted them, motivations, challenges, concerns, needs that are not being met, and possibly include a photo of your child.

During the meeting, be sure to:

- Avoid feeling intimidated when you walk into the meeting room, as the entire EMT most likely will be in attendance. While it may seem overwhelming to walk into a room full of educational professionals, it is important to remember that everyone attending shares one common goal: to provide your child/adolescent with the tools and environment necessary for their individualized success.

- Have all your documentation and questions ready to share.

- Have note-taking materials. Take note of who is in attendance, roles, action steps/by whom and when will these be completed, and other relevant comments made in the meeting.

- Write down the team member names/roles during formal introductions.

- Share your concerns and observations when prompted by the team.

- Be prepared to hear from the team (their observations, the child's educational history, medical history if you provided this information prior to the meeting, discussion of eligibility, etc.).

- Understand that eligibility meetings may not include the actual development of an initial plan. In some cases, the development of a treatment plan takes place in a separate meeting that is scheduled within an appropriate time frame after the eligibility meeting.

- Be prepared to sign the treatment plan. You may request to review the plan, sign, and return within a few days, if need be. Some signatures may be required to simply acknowledge that you were a part of the meeting, not that you agree to the treatment plan.

- Express your thoughts, share ideas for goals and means to reach them, and discuss any hesitations with/adjustments you'd like to see to any goals or accommodations recommended by the team.

- Remember that you are a highly valued member of the team, and they prefer you share thoughts, concerns, questions, etc.

Based on the diagnosis, data, and information gathered during the meeting, a treatment plan will be put into place. These plans could consist of:

- An informal accommodation plan, which generally is created to (1) gather data in order to determine next steps, or (2) support youth who display tendencies toward a specific diagnosis or need, but who do not formally fit the criteria for diagnosis or formal plans.

- A 504 plan, which usually is coordinated by the school counselor.

- An Individualized Education Plan, which usually is managed by the school resource team.

- An Individualized Healthcare Plan (IHP), which can also be embedded into a 504 or IEP when the diagnosis includes a physical disability or health impairment (in this case, the school nurse should be included in determining elements of a treatment plan).

- Note that if your requests for a plan are denied, you may appeal the decision. You may choose to contact your school administration and/or the district to gain information on that process within your region.

The table below describes basic distinctions between a 504, an IEP, and an IHP:

504	IEP	IHP
Eligible for students with any disability that: 1. impacts their ability to access the curriculum 2. substantially limits one or more of the basic life skills indicated in Section 504 of the Rehabilitation Act of 1973	Eligible for students who: 1. have one or more of the disabilities listed in IDEA 2. are significantly affected in their ability and/or educational performance within the general education curriculum	Eligible for students who require specialized medical care that does not impact educational performance or ability to access the curriculum
Accommodations can generally be provided in the classroom	Special education and related services generally are provided both in the homeroom and in pull-out classroom settings	Care plan for all school settings as determined by risk due to disability or impairment
Legally binding via Section 504 of the Rehabilitation Act of 1973	Legally binding via IDEA	Not legally binding
Typically reviewed annually (or more often if needed), but regulations state that a review once every three years is acceptable (Wright, 2008)	Reviewed annually (or more often if needed and if parents request) and reevaluated for eligibility every three years	Reviewed annually (or more often if needed and if parents request)

Summary

The DSM-5 evolved from a mere collection of statistical information for the U.S. Census in 1840 to being the world's standard tool for evaluating and diagnosing mental health disorders in children, adolescents, and adults. Numerous assessment tools have been devised to help in diagnosis determination. A few of these measures include the DISC, behavior rating report forms, cognitive tests, and achievement tests. Besides providing mental health professionals with more comprehensive information during the evaluation process, these tools also help produce thorough evaluations that lead to more accurate diagnoses. This information enables treatment providers to create and develop therapeutic, successful treatment plans for youth who require mental health services.

>>> QUICK RECAP

DSM-5 and Assessment Tools:

➢ The DSM (*Diagnostic Statistical Manual of Mental Disorders*), a clinical diagnostic tool used by clinicians, has undergone a series of revisions as more is learned about mental health.

➢ The DSM-5 is the most recently revised version of the DSM.

➢ The DSM-5 has both proponents and critics.

➢ The ICD-10 and ICD-11 are universal diagnostic tools that have been updated to work in conjunction with the DSM-5.

➢ There are a number of reputable and reliable assessment tools that are often used to supplement the DSM, including:

- Psychological assessment
- Neuropsychological assessment
- Educational assessment
- Achievement assessment

➢ Only trained professionals using valid and reliable measurements can diagnose. Self-diagnosis must not be a determining factor in diagnosis.

➢ Proper diagnosis is essential in creating effective individualized treatment plans.

(Cont.)

**Supporting Parents in the Initial Steps
of Determining Diagnosis:**

- Determine what the main issue is first – learning disability, behavioral health, or mental health concern.

- Encourage parents to reach out. School, pediatricians, and mental health professionals can provide solid information and next steps.

- Encourage parents to research, consider professional evaluations and assessments, and rule out all possibilities (physical, mental, and social-emotional deficiencies or needs).

- Explain the school meeting and evaluation process, what to expect, time frames, and how to prepare.

Chapter 2

Individualizing Treatment Plans

In order to develop effective and successful treatment plans for youth, treatment providers must take into account the many individual factors that make up a young person's life. Just as a cookie needs more than simply a few cups of flour to become the perfect sweet bite, a treatment plan needs more than a basic conception of the youth for whom it is being created to maximize its effectiveness. While a quality cookie requires sugar, eggs, butter, and vanilla, an effective and quality treatment plan requires attention to developmental, cultural, behavioral, emotional, social, genetic, and biological variables. Individualized treatment plans also require intentional consideration of various components that may currently be affecting the youth, such as recent life changes or other distinctive events that may have a significant impact. Attention to these two variables – the factors that provide insight into the whole child and any events or major life changes that could significantly impact the youth – leads to the holistic understanding required to create a treatment plan that meets the unique needs of a youth. This chapter presents brief overviews of several of the variables previously listed and provides examples of how they can be incorporated into social skill treatment planning.

Developmental Considerations

A youth's developmental level plays a huge role in constructing an appropriate treatment plan. Knowledge of typical development provides an idea of when particular skills generally emerge, what skills are most appropriate to target, and the best way to teach skills. Many theories have been devised to describe development in multiple areas, including cognition, morals, identity, language, socioemotional, social, psychosexual, and attachment. In this section, we highlight how to consider development when planning social skill instruction.

(The table on the next page highlights common theories of development. For more detailed information on these and other theories, see *A Child's World: Infancy through Adolescence* by Papalia, Olds, and Feldman (2005), or other similar resources.)

Middle Childhood (6-12 years)	Adolescence (12-18 years)
Psychosocial Stage of Development (Erikson, 1963) *Industry vs. Inferiority*	Psychosocial Stage of Development (Erikson, 1963) *Identity vs. Role Confusion*
Cognitive Stage of Development (Piaget, 1952) *Concrete Operational*	Cognitive Stage of Development (Piaget, 1952) *Formal Operational*
Moral Stage of Development (Kohlberg, 1981) *Conformity and Interpersonal Accord Authority and Social Order*	Moral Stage of Development (Kohlberg, 1981) *Social Contract*
Identity Development, Marcia et al., 1993 *Diffusion, Foreclosure, Moratorium, Achievement*	
Sample Milestones in this Stage: *Understands cause and effect Requires more concrete information Understands consequences Outward focus (others, rewards)*	Sample Milestones in this Stage: *Uses logic and complex thought Abstract and hypothetical thinking Motivated by peers and socialization Inward focus (self, appearance, identity)*

*While the theories listed above are widely used to describe general stages of development, it is important to note that these descriptions may not take cultural, gender, or individual context into consideration. Criticisms for each theory should be researched before including them as part of the baseline data for a treatment plan.

Treatment providers must consider a youth's developmental level when determining whether a social skill deficit exists. For example, children in early childhood are known for fairly egocentric thought – thinking that others' experiences are similar to their own. When this is the case, children, given their developmental level, would not be expected to be able to identify how their actions affect others. By late childhood and early adolescence, however, this skill should be acquired, so an absence of empathy might be seen as a social skill deficit. A youth's developmental level will play a large role in determining whether the absence of a skill is an indication of abnormal development or an age-appropriate deficit.

Developmental level also will guide what skills to target for treatment. In Chapter 5, "Social Skill Charts for Specific Mental Health Disorders," skills are listed in order from "basic" to "complex." Some of the more complex skills ("Budgeting and Managing Money," "Using Strategies to Find a Job," etc.) would not be appropriate goals to include in the treatment plans of younger children. To the same degree, it is essential that basic skills are mastered before their associated intermediate skills are taught and that intermediate skills are acquired prior to training in the advanced skills with which those intermediate skills are in-line with. This may mean a delay in teaching some of the skills suggested for particular mental health disorders until other aligned targeted basic skills are developed. For example, a person would need to learn the skill of "Talking with Others" (basic skill) before they could learn the skill of "Contributing to a Discussion" (complex skill). The main point to consider here is whether a targeted skill needs to build upon another more basic skill. Misreading needs, not recognizing gaps in key basic skills, or attempts to bypass teaching more basic skills in order to meet advanced-level goals could result in frustration, confusion, larger disparities in skills, and possibly a regression in skill level. Therefore, it is important that treatment providers continuously assess, reflect, evaluate, maintain patience, and ensure mastery of more basic skills before moving to more advanced skills that build upon basic needs ("data, data, data" is the name of the game).

Finally, a youth's developmental level will play a role in how skills are taught. For example, the social skill instruction model used at Boys Town requires youth to have attained a certain level of language and cognitive development. Youth who possess low cognitive functioning and/or poor language skills would be better served by treatment programs that use less language-based teaching and more behaviorally based teaching. Youth who perform at lower cognitive ranges can benefit from social skill training taught through the Boys Town Model, but accommodations should be considered. In Boys Town residential Family Homes, one such accommodation to the social skills model is a token economy system. This combines the social skill training model with a behavioral motivation system that helps produce optimal results. Learning occurs at both the verbal and behavioral level. Another possible accommodation for youth with lower cognitive functioning would include providing social skill cards that include steps and pictures that help youth learn the skills. Using these cards also could earn rewards for youth via a motivation system. Conversely, youth with average intellect may not necessarily require as many prompts and cues for learning to take place.

There are many forms of development to consider when creating individualized treatment plans. In this section, we briefly touched on development areas that should be considered when using the Boys Town Model. A youth's developmental level will ultimately guide treatment providers as they determine which skill deficit to address, what social skills to choose for instruction, and how best to teach these skills.

Cultural Considerations

The ADDRESSING Model is a tool that can help formulate culturally responsive treatment methods that better serve children and families by recognizing and respecting their individual identities. ADDRESSING is an acronym that stands for **A**ge and generational influences, **D**evelopmental and acquired **D**isabilities, **R**eligion and spiritual orientation, **E**thnicity, **S**ocioeconomic status, **S**exual orientation, **I**ndigenous heritage, **N**ational origin, and **G**ender. This tool can help treatment providers understand the important role culture plays in a youth's development and account for cultural groups and influences. The focus of this approach is to look at how each individual's multicultural background influences knowledge, skills, and attitudes about their external and internal worlds. ADDRESSING, as the acronym implies, is designed to prevent treatment providers from making inaccurate or sweeping generalizations based on surface-level characteristics and internalized beliefs. It's a model for understanding the way cultural influences affect one's worldview in addition to recognizing the various cultural influences that help shape and explain a person's identity. While this is a critical step in developing the right care and treatment plan, those who may not have strong cultural awareness, knowledge, and skills may view certain populations or people through a flawed, distorted, or unfair lens. Therefore, it is essential that treatment providers develop their cultural responsiveness by continually learning about other cultures and beliefs, identifying biases, and assessing their own cultural perspectives (Hays, 2008).

What Is the Impact?

When social skill instruction is part of an individualized treatment plan, cultural and ethnic factors will influence what skills are targeted, how those skills are taught, and what skill components are included. For example, many cultures consider it a sign of disrespect for a youth to make direct eye contact with an adult. However, almost all of the social skills taught in the Boys Town Model include the component, "Look at the person." Therefore, when teaching this specific behavior to a youth who may have been taught to avoid eye contact, a caregiver may need to modify or target it for extra teaching and shape it over a longer period of time. The caregiver also should teach discrimination skills to the youth, helping them to understand that it is acceptable to look at their teacher at school or boss at work, but it may not be appropriate to make eye contact with elders who are from or share their culture. Other behavioral areas that may require modified goals because of culture-specific factors or influences (family, home life, economic class, ethnicity, etc.) include the following:

- Body and facial gestures

- Social coolness versus warmth

- Following directions (as opposed to seeing it as a request or an option)

- Tone and volume

- Personal space

- Displays of emotion

- Patterns of communication in various situations

- Manners

- Courtesy

- Roles (student, teacher, male, female, age, etc.)

- Sense of fairness and justice

Support and understanding are key when teaching youth skills that may step outside their comfort level or defy the cultural expectations taught within their household. Treatment providers should appreciate how a youth's culture has influenced their beliefs, behaviors, and values. Moreover, treatment providers should demonstrate respect for the youth's culture and avoid undermining norms instilled at home while simultaneously supporting the development of these new skills. This can be done in a variety of ways, including...

- Acknowledging the importance of their current social norm within specific contexts.

- Discussing the value of their norm in specific contexts.

- Brainstorming together times/settings where the new skill would be valuable and more fitting.

- Using observational data to demonstrate or model to them the value of this new skill within certain contexts.

- Getting the family involved by asking for their support and knowledge to help the youth understand when the new skill is appropriate and when the cultural norm is appropriate. Gaining their insight and working with them can ensure the youth learns the new skill while staying true to their cultural norms.

As stated earlier, treatment providers should be comfortable with understanding their own cultural identities, values, and biases so that they can be more proactive and effective with the youth they are serving. Additionally, treatment providers should be willing to practice ongoing and consistent critical self-reflection in order to ensure that cultural differences do not lead to care and treatment goals that do not align with the youth's needs. Treatment providers could begin by recognizing their own identity within the boundaries of the ADDRESSING framework and how these features shape their viewpoints and interactions. Once this understanding of self is in place, it may be easier to ask reflective questions when addressing youth needs, such as:

- Do I have any preconceived notions about this youth?

- Do my expectations coordinate with the youth's previous experiences, background, and household norms, or do I need to readjust to meet the youth where they currently are?

- Am I educated enough about the youth's cultural background (household culture and communal culture)?

- Where or from whom can I gather more information to make informed decisions on social skills goals?

In addition to asking self-reflective questions – Am I educated enough about the youth's cultural background (household culture and communal culture)? Where or from whom can I gather more information to make informed decisions on social skills goals? – is the importance of understanding the impact of new skills on a youth's self-identity within their cultural lens. When teaching social skills, it is essential that treatment providers evaluate how learning a new set of skills will affect youth self-identity, both inside and outside the treatment setting. Those who feel accepted and develop a sense of belonging may begin to culturally identify and connect deeply with treatment providers and other youth within the treatment setting. This deep sense of connection and belonging could foster a stronger confidence and security in self, thus leading to more healthy risk-taking behaviors (e.g., participation, engagement, and friendship-seeking). Conversely, those who feel they are being forced to acculturate into the traditional American mainstream or who feel less accepted by their peers may resist treatment or possibly adopt counterproductive behaviors in response (e.g., meltdowns or tantrums, disengagement, shutting down, or emotional reactivity). Careful and consistent evaluation, frequent check-ins with the youth, and adapting goals accordingly will result in more positive outcomes.

Finally, culturally competent treatment providers should be aware that culture, race, and ethnicity are not to be used interchangeably as each has a distinct meaning. Culture has shared elements, including language, history, and geographic location, but there is no biological link. It can be broadly defined as the learned characteristics and way of life of a group of people, including social norms, traditions, and values. Many identify as multicultural, as they belong to a variety of cultural groups. These groups could include heritage, social groups, and ethnic groups, to name a few.

Race is based on geography and physical characteristics (skin color, facial features, etc.) that tend to be genetically related. Race often is an aspect of an individual's self-identification, but it offers little information about the person. For example, race may identify one's social heritage but it clarifies little in terms of an individual's educational level, cultural context, or current environment. When formulating a treatment plan, knowledge of a youth's race can help treatment providers determine whether the youth considers themself to be part of the dominant or minority culture and the impact that will have on treatment goals.

Ethnicity tends to tie into nationality. It includes heritage, ancestry, history, and culture (norms, beliefs, dialect, cuisine, arts, etc.). Ethnicity also formulates many labels and perceptions that are not necessarily true for all members who may belong to the same ethnic group (Hays, 2008). Therefore, as stated earlier, it is vital that treatment providers actively reflect on their own cultural biases, possible stereotypes or underlying assumptions, and actively seek information to understand the youth as a whole before determining plans for treatment.

It is also important to note that many youth identify within multiple races, ethnic affiliations, and/or cultures (via internal change, diffusion, etc.). Add to this unique household norms and recent cultural and societal shifts and it is easy to see that race, ethnicity, and culture identification should act as a "penciled in" blueprint rather than a "permanent marker" final product. Treatment providers must avoid adopting fixed ideas of cultures, races, and ethnicities. Instead, they must be comfortable asking questions, researching, and gaining an understanding of the individual.

Including All Children's Unique Needs

Boys Town has always adhered to the goal of individualized, appropriate, relevant, and sensitive treatment for all children regardless of race, gender, faith or religion, and physical, mental, and intellectual ability. Each child has an individualized treatment plan with social skills that are tailored to fit the unique background and specific needs of that child. The Boys Town Social Skills Curriculum uses inclusive language and features several skills that reflect the diversity of children and their needs. Only in this way can fair and effective care for all youth, regardless of race, gender, faith, religion, or ability, be achieved. To include the unique needs for all children, treatment providers should add these two important questions to their care, treatment, and social skills planning activities:

- Due to the child's culture, gender, faith or religion, and ability, are there any special teaching strategies or social skills we need to explore and utilize?

- Are we teaching sufficient skill variations that will lead to success in the child's own culture, environment, and society at large?

Knowledge of different cultures, genders, faiths, religions, and physical, mental, and intellectual abilities is essential for effective care and treatment. Treatment providers need to become aware of the experiences, values, and lifestyles inherent to all these critical areas unique to each child. Only in this way can we expect to have a positive impact on the care and development of all children.

Behavioral and Emotional Considerations

Emotion and behavior are two distinctly individualistic variables to take into account when developing individualized treatment plans. Youth with behavioral and/or emotional problems generally require clearly targeted and defined treatment goals related to social skills, as many social skills deficits can potentially be a cause and/or effect of a mental health disorder. While social skills goals are important when developing individualized treatment plans for youth with behavior and/or emotional problems, it is also important to address other aspects of behavioral and emotional problems. Such aspects become clear when referral concerns and symptoms are analyzed because they tend to be related. At times, the treatment team may need to consider supplementing the IEP with a Functional Behavior Assessment (FBA) and Behavioral Intervention Plan (BIP). These tools are useful in identifying a specific problem behavior and/or emotion, measuring present levels, and determining triggers or purpose of the identified problem behavior and/or emotion. Once the behavior and/or emotion is understood via a FBA, the team can then create a BIP, which provides the appropriate skills, tools, and supports to address the behaviors identified in the FBA.

One clear example of how individual behavioral and emotional considerations come into play can be seen by looking at youth who experience externalizing disorders versus internalizing disorders. Externalizing disorders, grouped within the heading of "Disruptive, Impulse-Control, and Conduct Disorders" in the DSM-5, include diagnoses like Oppositional Defiant Disorder and Conduct Disorder, while internalizing disorders include diagnoses like Generalized Anxiety Disorder and Major Depressive Disorder. Youth diagnosed with externalizing disorders tend to display maladaptive conduct toward their environment and may be more likely to express themselves through their behaviors. Youth with internalizing disorders tend to turn inwards, avoid communicating issues with others, and may be more likely to express themselves through language or other more reserved means. This provides an indication of the best way to teach social skills to particular youth. For example, youth who are diagnosed with an externalizing disorder may respond better to short and direct instructions, while youth diagnosed with internalizing disorders may respond more readily to directives that include lengthy rationales and empathetic statements. Each youth is different, but identifying broad emotional and behavioral styles will help predict responses to different forms of instruction.

Another significant behavioral consideration is the youth's learning history. A learning history includes the behaviors that have been trained, shaped, reinforced, and punished. Examination and consideration of the learning history will help treatment providers to better understand what goals need to be accomplished and how to best achieve those goals. To illustrate, consider a thirteen-year-old boy who has grown up in a household where arguing is reinforced with attention (either positive attention in that his request is granted or negative attention in that he gains feedback in any capacity regardless of the type of feedback). Conversely, appropriate requests made by this thirteen-year-old, without residual argumentative behaviors, are essentially ignored. This behavior is then reinforced in the classroom when teachers and peers provide attention (be it positive or negative) when the boy is argumentative. It will take this youth much longer to learn the skill of "Accepting 'No' for an Answer" because of a learning history that has punished this behavior by means of ignoring, while at the same time reinforcing a behavior of arguing for desired outcomes. It is important for treatment providers to keep factors such as learned behaviors in mind when working with youth so they are able to set realistic time frames for treatment goals. To determine the learning history of a youth, data can be collected via caregiver interview, teacher interview, observations, direct inquiry discussion with the youth (if appropriate), or other means.

Naturally, some youth will have learning histories in which appropriate skills that are suggested for particular disorders have in fact been reinforced. In these cases, there most likely will not be a deficit of reinforced skills. Therefore, they may not need to be taught or trained. When this circumstance arises, the treatment providers should consider why the youth fails to demonstrate the appropriate skill, as certain behaviors and emotions may serve a particular function in their life. For example, a lack of motivation or ability to display the appropriate skill even after training and reinforcement could serve the purpose of...

- Gaining something of value to the youth (e.g., attention from adults or peers, or relative stability within their home by behaving in a particular manner).

- Avoiding an undesired outcome if the appropriate skill is displayed (e.g., getting out of trouble or out of performing an unwanted task).

- Avoiding incorrectly displaying the appropriate skill (performance anxiety).

- Minimizing the potential for other variables or obstacles to impede the youth's ability to demonstrate the skill.

Consider a boy diagnosed with Oppositional Defiant Disorder. A common symptom associated with this disorder is deliberately annoying others. A thorough assessment might reveal that the youth pinches his sister and swears at his mother for the purpose of gaining their attention, and that he lacks the proper skills to communicate his desire for attention and connection in a more acceptable manner. Not only will this youth need to be taught the social skill of "Getting Another Person's Attention," but his family also will need to be taught how to withhold negative attention when he uses annoying behaviors and offer positive attention when he displays appropriate skills of engagement. Family coaching and support can be achieved by building strong relationships between the school and home, clearly and consistently communicating goals, thoroughly explaining and modeling how caregivers can offer positive attention when the youth appropriately seeks attention, and by providing parent-child interaction training or other means of parent-enrichment training.

A youth's level of emotional development also comes into play when outlining individualized treatment. Emotional expression is on a continuum, with some individuals being extremely emotional and others exhibiting no emotion. For example, individuals with Autism Spectrum Disorder tend to have a limited emotional range and might seem to exhibit an overall "flat" affect. This disorder-associated skill deficit may require the treatment provider to focus on more foundational elements to build on, such as "Identifying Your Own Feelings" or "Making Eye Contact," before working on the next level of basic skills, such as "Showing Sensitivity to Others."

Other individuals may be on the opposite end of the continuum, where intensity of emotion and ease of arousal are issues. This might be the case for youth who are diagnosed with a Mood Disorder, such as Disruptive Mood Dysregulation Disorder, or a diagnosis that falls under the heading of "Disruptive, Impulse-Control, and Conduct Disorders." For these youth, teaching a social skill like "Controlling Emotions" will be essential. Within the scope of this central goal lies specific supplementary targets that could include cultivation of appropriate emotional expression, education on the impact of emotional expression on relationships and, in some cases, training on the significance of medication in regulating emotions.

As explained earlier, extreme emotions and behaviors are associated with many DSM-5 diagnoses. Some aspects of emotion and behavior to consider include:

- *Development* – developmental level, development of the behavior and/or emotional response, and overall development of the whole child

- *Range* – the variation between behavioral and/or emotional extremes

- *Intensity* – the magnitude of behavior and/or emotion

- *Duration* – how long the extreme behavior and/or emotion lasts

- *Frequency* – how often the behavior and/or emotion occurs

- *Form* – manifestation

- *Function* – the purpose served by the behavior and/or emotion usually associated with acquirement or avoidance

- *Cultural Expectations* – how the youth's overall and household background may impact emotional and/or behavioral responses

- *History* – learning history of the youth and any learned behaviors that may have resulted

A treatment plan that addresses all of these dimensions increases the likelihood that emotional and behavioral symptoms associated with a youth's diagnosis are successfully reduced and replaced with more appropriate and healthy behaviors.

Social Considerations

A youth's physical, emotional, and behavioral functioning can be greatly affected by ecological circumstances. These include, but are not limited to, family, school, peers, socioeconomic status, religion/church, and community. Social environment and mesospheric influences (described later in this chapter) play a large role in defining an individual, and provide a context for understanding an individual's past and current behavior. The impact of social factors cannot be overlooked when constructing a truly individualized treatment plan.

When assessing a youth and developing a treatment plan, the treatment provider should look for positive social variables as well as risk factors. For example, youth from lower-income families generally experience little power within the exosystems that they encounter, like education or health systems. Often, these youth witness their caregivers' frustrations and struggles, which can create a sense of hopelessness, uncertainty, and instability, as if external forces are controlling their lives. These types of social experiences can influence a youth's sense of security and trust, which in turn affects how they respond to treatment and to those who provide it. For this reason, older youth should be involved in the development of their treatment plans, as involvement provides them with a sense of control and ownership.

As a youth develops and progresses through life, they encounter a number of influential forces, such as parents/caregivers, siblings, teachers, and peers. These forces play a role (be it big or small) in shaping their social growth through reinforcement, punishment, and modeling. Youth also acquire a wide breadth of social knowledge and responses by observing and imitating their parents'/caregivers', siblings', and peers' behaviors, as well as by imitating behaviors observed on social media and other cultural influences. This valuable information teaches youth social norms, rules, and ways to interact with others. While this social knowledge attainment may not always be prosocial, it may help them survive within their environment or get their physiological needs met. This is apparent when working with youth, for example, who have been involved in gangs. Typically, youth report that gang involvement provides prestige and safety within their community. Although this involvement is not desirable in mainstream society, some within the youth's community may view it as a protective mechanism (Walker-Barnes & Mason, 2001).

Youth are clearly affected by family members' responses to their behavior, whether they are living at home or in a treatment program. That is why families should be involved in treatment planning and supporting new skills youth learn through treatment. For example, parents of all youth who are involved in Boys Town residential treatment programs are required to complete parenting courses. When implementing social skill instruction, it is crucial that the family is informed about skills the youth is learning and how best to support the youth so they can better learn and master those skills. This partnership between treatment providers and family, however, can be difficult to foster and maintain. Reasons for complications in treatment provider-home relations can stem from a number of factors, including:

- lack of communication and/or attempts to communicate with the family early on

- lack of clarity in expectations or in overall communications sent home

- general distrust of treatment providers

- a sense of being unwelcome by the institution in which the treatment providers work

- language barriers

- cultural barriers (e.g., some cultures may not highly value this relationship, while other cultures may see communicating with staff as "stepping over a line" and disrespectful)

- logistics, meaning some caregivers are simply too busy and are trying to stay afloat with their daily schedules

- fears of being burdensome, getting in the way, or looking uneducated and/or incapable

- negative past experiences with previous support systems

To counter these factors and to foster a healthy partnership with families, treatment providers can take small, but meaningful steps that encourage family engagement. The first step in cultivating this partnership involves the act of committing to family involvement and maintenance of a healthy partnership. Once treatment providers have made this commitment, they can focus on setting clear expectations for family communications and on opening the trusted avenue for families to do the same. This can be done by:

- listening to families and gaining a sense of underlying causes for possible disengagement or mistrust

- matching individualized resources and supports to families based on needs

- making the criticality of their presence well-known by showcasing how their support is monumental in the success of their child, how they offer unique perspective, advocacy, and insight, and how they can reach the youth on a level that no other team player could

- opening multiple modes of communication, paying special attention to specific family needs in terms of communication method, language, time frames for communication, and ease of communication

- maintaining accessibility for the family

- connecting through home visits where appropriate or through community engagements

Treatment providers could also follow what the National PTA has coined "the Four I's": inclusion (embrace and value multiple perspectives), individualization (address unique family and youth needs), impact (empower families), and integration (align with the educational system) (National PTA, 2019). Family partnerships and shared responsibility can strengthen family dynamics and youth outcomes.

Peers also exert a large influence on the behavior of youth. Consider the relationship between peer groups and school performance. When a youth's peers do not value academic and behavioral achievement, they will have a negative effect on how the youth behaves and performs at school. For example, consider a youth who is diagnosed with Attention-Deficit/Hyperactivity Disorder (ADHD). The youth may clearly need to learn the skill of "Doing Good Quality Work." However, further assessment might indicate that the youth does not take their time to complete schoolwork because of peer pressure, as peers either hurriedly complete their work or refuse to do it. They also tease youth who take their work seriously. This information can guide the treatment provider to teach target skills like "Resisting Peer Pressure" and "Responding to Teasing that's Hurtful," in addition to "Doing Good Quality Work."

Social microsystem factors encompass a myriad of variables, including family, peers, and community. All of these variables play a significant role in youth development and behavior. They affect the skills that youth deem as important and the skills that youth have learned. Social context provides an overall understanding of where youth are coming from, which helps guide how treatment should proceed.

Genetic and Biological Considerations

Most psychologists today generally agree that genetics and biology play just as important a role in human behavior as environment. Many mental health disorder diagnoses have been linked to genetic causes. Particular cases of intellectual disabilities like Down's syndrome and Fragile X are caused by genetic syndromes. The biology of individuals with particular disorders such as ADHD and Anorexia Nervosa (Mash & Barkley, 2007) also has been found to be different. This research-based understanding highlights the importance of genetic and biological factors in the expression and progression of symptoms, and social skills deficits are no exception.

Given the influence that genetic and biological factors have on social skill deficits, it is crucial to include medical professionals as members of any treatment team. Medical professionals like pediatricians and psychiatrists can offer specialized information regarding biologically based aspects of treatment planning. For example, medication is a common treatment plan component when addressing ADHD. When medication is part of a treatment plan, it is essential to involve a doctor who can monitor medication side effects and effectiveness, as these medication-related factors can greatly impact the treatment of all facets of a youth's life. Another example would be youth who are diagnosed with eating disorders; these disorders can be life threatening if they are not addressed medically. In fact, hospitalization, medication, and/or nutritional counseling may be necessary. In cases where the primary goal of treatment is medically related, social skill instruction still plays an important supporting role by improving diagnosis-related social skill deficits. Acquiring or strengthening social skills such as "Seeking Professional Assistance," for example, could be a necessary part of the plan.

When working with youth who have DSM-5 diagnoses, it is essential that treatment providers clearly articulate the role that biology (such as imbalances and brain dysfunction) and genetics (such as epigenetic trauma, genetic variation, family history and genetic heritability, and genetic polymorphisms) play in symptoms experienced. When a youth is educated on how these factors play into their diagnosis and the accompanying symptoms, the more likely they will: (a) accept the diagnosis and understand symptoms involved, (b) avoid self-blame, shame, or self-doubt, (c) gain confidence and sense of self, (d) gain a sense of connection knowing that they are not alone in the diagnostic symptoms, and (e) feel more confidence in the ability to overcome symptoms. It is important to note that, just as when determining the complexity of social skill goals in a treatment plan, treatment providers should keep developmental and cognitive considerations at the forefront when determining the dosage and depth of this education.

Just as important as education is in the role of biology and genetics, so too is ensuring that youth are made aware of their own power in countering these factors via brain plasticity and effective effort. There is a saying that "our genetics and biology are not our destiny." Youth should understand that they are not limited by their biology and that they are capable of learning how to cope with it effectively. Often, this process involves learning social skills, which is what makes skills teaching such a valuable treatment component. (We caution providers to avoid the pitfall of allowing youth to believe they are helpless in the control of their symptoms. Even with disorders that are largely treated by medication, youth still have the responsibility of taking their medication in order to access the ability to reach further goals, all of which are very much within their control.)

Biological factors provide a framework for performance. Even biological elements like metabolic rates, digestion, and sleep can cause and interact with symptoms associated with many DSM-5 diagnoses. Treatment providers also should remember to consider how general medical conditions can influence mental health, as some physical conditions can mimic or exacerbate mental problems. For example, several symptoms associated with hypothyroidism (sluggishness, tiredness, slow speech, negative affect, and reduced appetite) resemble symptoms that also are associated with depression. If possible physical causes are not ruled out through consulting with a youth's physician, hypothyroidism symptoms could be mistaken for symptoms of depression. In some cases, medical tests might be needed before a mental health diagnosis can be made. For example, youth who have encopresis should undergo medical tests to determine if constipation is the cause of soiling. If these youth are found to have constipation, the condition may require more medical intervention than if constipation was absent.

Genetic and biological factors are continuously operating within us. These factors affect us at varying levels and interact with the environment to produce a unique whole that forms mental health. The astute treatment provider is wise to include both individual genetic and biological histories and current biological functioning when making treatment planning decisions. In addition, providers should be ready and willing to include medical professionals, including pediatricians and specialists, in treatment planning discussions in order to develop fully informed plans.

Bioecological Theory

Bronfenbrenner's bioecological theory of development, an extension based on his original ecological model of development, provides a framework for understanding the whole child. This framework can be beneficial when creating an individualized treatment plan. The model consists of nested systems that make up the interactions and influences on a child's life. Ordered in terms of proximity and direct influence, Bronfenbrenner labeled these systems as:

1. **Microsystem:** closest spheres of influence, such as family, neighborhood, friends, school community, and coaches

2. **Mesosystem:** interactions between two microsystems within the child's life, such as home-to-school interactions

3. **Exosystem:** indirect influences of structures within the microsystem, such as family finances, school board, media, government

4. **Macrosystem:** ideologies and attitudes, such as cultural values, laws, norms, and religion

5. **Chronosystem:** interaction between the child and systems, between the systems themselves, and the change/growth in all of these elements over time

The final piece to the bioecological framework is the Process-Person-Context-Time Model (PPCT), which focuses on the interactions between these systems (Bronfenbrenner & Ceci, 1994). In the context of this theory:

1. Process refers to proximal processes, meaning the development of constant and systemic interaction between the child and their environment.

2. Person refers to the characteristics of the child. The three most notable characteristics being:

   a. Demand characteristics: age, gender, physical attributes

   b. Resource characteristics: mental, emotional, and material resources

   c. Force characteristics: motivation, temperament

3. Context refers to the five nested ecological systems and how they impact a child's development.

4. Time refers to three distinct moments:

   a. Micro-time, or specific moments of proximal processes

   b. Meso-time, or the extent to which the processes occur

   c. Macro-time, or the bidirectional growth and change of cultural ideologies and attitudes

While this model provides a general framework for understanding the whole child or adolescent, it may also lead to broad assumptions and possible misrepresentations of an individual based on those assumptions. Therefore, it is important that an individual's culture, character, and core are taken into consideration.

Summary

When developing individualized treatment plans, it's essential to take into account the many factors that influence and shape youth and their behavior. There are developmental, cultural, behavioral, emotional, social, genetic, and biological factors that are unique to each and every youth. Some of these factors will play more prominent roles than others in a youth's treatment. But, all these factors need to be carefully considered from the beginning in order to create an effective treatment plan that has the best opportunity to succeed.

>>> QUICK RECAP

Individualizing Treatment Plans:

➤ **Developmental Considerations:** Age and developmental skill levels should be taken into account when determining deficits present, appropriate skills to be taught, and methods/approaches to social skills training.

➤ **Cultural Considerations:** The ADDRESSING framework, understanding of one's cultural biases and its impact on treatment, ongoing cultural competency education and personal work for treatment providers, and recognition of how individual culture impacts social skills should be taken into account when planning treatment.

➤ **Behavioral and Emotional Considerations:** Awareness of externalizing vs. internalizing vs. mixed diagnosis and symptom-specific social skills deficits when creating and implementing treatment plans. FBA's may be considered, as well.

➤ **Biological and Genetic Considerations:** Youth should be educated on how these factors impact them, as well as how they can overcome these factors in treatment planning.

➤ **Bioecological Spheres:** Microsystem, mesosystem, exosystem, macrosystem, chronosystem, and PPCT should be taken into consideration. However, broad generalizations based on these spheres and the interactions between them should be avoided.

Chapter 3

Foundational Key Steps Toward a Successful Treatment Plan

The previous chapter identified important considerations in the initial stages of treatment planning. These considerations are important because they greatly influence a youth's development and behavior, how they perceive the world around them, and how they process new information. This chapter shifts the focus from considerations regarding the youth in question to considerations regarding treatment providers and the team working to provide individualized support. Foundational keys that guide treatment teams toward a successful plan, such as data collection, communication, effective collaborative effort, and strategic and tactical goals, are examined.

Ideas for Data Collection When Trying to Understand the Whole Child

As stated earlier, there are a number of individualized variables that need to be considered in the initial stages of treatment planning. The information needed to analyze these variables may, and should be, collected in a variety of ways. Listed below are some data collection points that can be gathered at school, at home, in professional settings, and within the community.

Possible data points from the school:

- Teacher, paraeducator, and specialist observations – informal accommodation data, progress monitoring data, behavioral observations, communication style with both peers and adults, preferences in learning, engagement level, emotional regulation and expression, social notes

- Lunch and recess aide observations – behavior and social patterns during unstructured times, introverts/extroverts/amniverts, group vs. individual play, reciprocal vs. vertical play, comfort in team vs. small-group play, high- or low-energy preference

- Educational history, test scores, and grades

- Absences, tardies

- Behavioral referrals

- Health room visits

- Special education testing

- Mental health evaluations

- Speech and language pathologist or audiology observations, if appropriate

- Counselor notes and observations

- Occupational therapist observations, if appropriate

- Physical therapist or mobility service observations, if appropriate
- Grade-level milestones
- Student input – academic preferences, school and home environment, attitudes, beliefs, values, social/gender/sexual/spiritual preferences, personality, most beneficial teacher style/ educational methods and supports

Possible data points from home:

- Routines and rules, schedules, norms at home
- Parenting style, belief system, traditions, family dynamics, attachment
- Family history
- History of academic, medical, and mental health needs in the family
- Who the youth is outside of the school setting – hobbies, traits, emotions, free time, orientations, etc.
- Relationships at home and within the community
- Team sports, clubs, and outside extracurriculars
- Past traumatic experiences or major life events
- Support systems in place
- Medical history
- Residential history – moves, neighborhoods
- Observational notes from caregivers, coaches, sponsors, club leaders, etc.

Possible data points from other professional settings:

- Psychological/neuropsychological assessments
- Cognitive aptitude assessments
- Therapist, psychologist, psychiatrist insights
- Occupational therapist insights
- Tutor observations
- Pediatrician notes and observations

There are a number of settings and contexts for data collection, each serving their own purpose and each providing focused insight. Multiple methods of data collection from various settings and contexts will enhance a treatment provider's understanding of the whole child, of individualized needs, and of approaches that may best meet these individualized needs.

Treatment Provider Commitment and Communication

The two Cs of team success in creating and maintaining a treatment plan are **commitment** and **communication**. Treatment providers must be committed to the youth, the plan, and to the goals that are housed within the plan. Clear and consistent communication is another "must" for success.

Commitment to the youth means that the treatment providers take time to get to know the whole child and use this information in treatment planning. Employing the elements discussed earlier in this chapter and maintaining a solid understanding of the youth's present levels, spheres and systems of influence, and progress is essential in maintaining an effective individualized treatment plan. Commitment to the plan involves being fully on-board and engaged in its creation and upkeep. Treatment providers should lend their insight, voice, and skills throughout the process. Thorough understanding of the plan and belief in the process is important, as well. Commitment to the goals that are housed within the plan entails agreement on each goal in alignment with individual needs, as well as on the specificities of each goal (measures, roles, time frames, method, etc.).

Communication is an absolute when it comes to team success in implementing an individualized treatment plan. Straightforward, articulate, and goal-oriented collaborative communication between treatment providers and all key stakeholders should be ongoing. Themes around purposeful communication may include:

- Roles

- Clarity of all moving parts and how everything should be moving together

- Information pertaining to progress, regression, possible factors contributing to change

- Insights, observations, questions, and ways to further collaborate

- Who/what/how to support parents and caregivers in maintaining continuity in the training and support of specified social skills goals between home, community, and institution (school, in-patient treatment program, etc.)

- Check-ins about the communication method to ensure it maintains its strength

- Self- and team-assessment of efficacy, understanding, impact, function, and contribution to treatment plan progress

- Sharing of information learned regarding the whole child to ensure everyone on the team is on the same level of understanding

Collaborative Effort of Stakeholders

Communication and commitment are paramount to treatment success. At times though, members of the treatment team may not be as in sync with the collaborative process as desired. Reasons for this could stem from a number of factors such as: lack of experience in effective collaborative teams, feeling inept or as if they do not have much to bring to the table, feeling overworked and overwhelmed, or any number of other influences that lend themselves to a limited synergetic flow.

Establishing effective, collaborative habits from the get-go lessens the possibility of this occurring. It sets the tone of a focused team that welcomes varying perspectives and that values all team members and their thoughts no matter how big or small those thoughts may seem in the moment. Treatment providers should strive to build a foundation of effective collaborative habits with their team members, as this leads to greater long-term outcomes.

Establishing Effective Collaboration Within the Treatment Team

At the onset of treatment planning, there are a number of ways to establish effective collaborative habits within the treatment team. Of these, a few solid and reliable means include:

Alignment: First and foremost, the team needs to be in alignment. This means that they have a common understanding of needs, the youth as a whole, roles and cohesion between roles, and expectations and goals. Additionally, teams should consider keeping organized and updated notes within shared documents to ensure clarity and alignment, and to ensure at least one written form of shared communication.

Communication: Internal communication methods should be clearly articulated and streamlined. This includes formal and informal communication modes, frequency of communication, and methods for team transparency so that all are in-the-know, as it is easy to fall into the habit of sharing with certain team members and not sharing with others. (This can be due to a number of reasons including convenience, schedule conflicts, comfort with team members, quantity of time spent with team members, etc.) Additionally, teams should consider revisiting their methods of communication to identify any obstacles or pain points and share what is working well in their communication system.

Collaborative behaviors: Treatment providers can spearhead effective collaboration within the team by modeling effective collaborative behaviors. This can include:

- following transformative leadership approaches

- being efficient in streams of action

- ensuring that each team member walks away feeling positive, heard, and with a solid understanding of action steps (both individual and cohesive action steps)

- being visible and present

- forging bonds between all team members

Forging bonds: By making an effort to build bonds within the team, treatment providers can stave off a number of issues that generally arise when multiple personalities and perspectives come together with a common goal. This can be done by:

- showing appreciation (praise, recognition, gratitude) for team members and specific contributions that they make, how these contributions impact the team, and how these contributions will continue to aid in treatment plan success

- carving out time to invite discussion about team member experiences, as well as what they need from the team

- ensuring that every member understands their value as well as the value of their teammates in treatment plan success

- actively listening to each other

- encouraging questions and creative thinking

- establishing trust by being transparent, nonjudgmental, and creating an inviting atmosphere

- encouraging the team to share disagreements, then addressing these disagreements immediately

When working with a team, it is inevitable that there will be some disagreements along the way. Unproductive or unsettled disagreements within the treatment team are another possible hindrance to effective collaboration. If a member of the treatment team leaves a disagreement unstated or feels that their dissent goes unheard, they may find themselves out of alignment with the team. They may lose focus of the mission, their role, their trust in the team, or their trust in the plan. At the same time, team members who attempt to solve disputes in an unproductive or adverse manner may find themselves in a similarly negative and obstructive situation. Both of these outcomes inhibit the opportunity to provide a successful treatment plan that can only be brought to life by a strong team. Effective conflict-resolution skills and respectful approaches to disagreements are significant in effective collaboration.

Exploring and Resolving Disputes that Arise in the Collaborative Process

Effective conflict resolution and respectful mediation of disagreements starts with the effective habits of collaboration outlined earlier. Once the foundations of collaborative effort have been established, team members will feel more comfortable sharing concerns and devising productive outcomes with each other. Some steps to navigate through disputes or disagreements as they arise in the collaborative process include:

Keep realistic reminders in mind: Disputes and disagreements are inevitable in the collaborative process. Team members are coming in with their own unique perspectives and systems of thought. In addition, each team member is a stakeholder in the youth for whom the treatment plan is being created. They care. They are there for one reason and that reason is to help the youth succeed. This can lead to big emotions, especially if they feel that something will hinder the success of the treatment plan or if they feel that their work is hindered or invalidated. Remember that disputes will arise, and that this is okay.

Encourage immediate articulation of disagreements or disputes: This is much easier when effective collaborative habits have been established. Treatment providers should encourage team members to express concerns as soon as possible, without worry of judgement, of angering others, or of looking like a naysayer.

Create a system: To further encourage communication of concern, a system could be put in place for sharing. One idea may include creating a formula for language used in sharing and exploring disagreements.

Another idea may include allocating time in meetings specifically for sharing concerns. Creating a system will help to diminish any worries of being seen in a negative light, of being reprimanded, or of being disparaged.

Model healthy disagreements: This could include treatment providers guiding teammates through disagreements by demonstrating active listening, summarizing concerns shared and checking for accuracy, asking curious questions, validating, and using resolution-oriented language to find an outcome in which everyone feels heard and positive about next steps.

Focus on the right thing: Ensure that team members keep their focus on their issues with the treatment plan, not on specific team members. Ensure that concerns do not turn into personal attacks or belittling comments. The dispute or disagreement should be clearly articulated and understood by all, and emotions should never replace logic and strategy in these moments. To this end, any conversations that may be veering toward blame, shame, or targeting individuals should be quickly diverted and brought back to the main issue.

Move forward and check in: Once a resolution has been established, the team should come up with a specific time in which they will check in regarding this specific piece.

Ensuring Goals Remain Relevant and Specific to Individual Needs

Just as fundamental as understanding every sphere and system that works together to create the whole youth is understanding how the youth's needs adjust, and then shifting course in order to meet those needs. Once an individualized treatment plan is in place, treatment providers have the responsibility of consistently monitoring and evaluating goals. Treatment goals should follow the S.M.A.R.T. acronym. Goals should be:

- **Specific** – Goals typically follow a formula that requires specificity of (a) time frame (by what date), (b) who (the youth), (c) what (specific desired action or behavior), (d) where (in what settings and contexts), (e) how often (percentage of times and accuracy of usage), (f) with (supports and tools that will be used to assist the youth), and (g) as determined by (which data collection tools and persons will be used to determine mastery).

- **Measurable** – Objective measures put in place should be (a) quantitative, (b) aligned with performance criteria of the goals (usually described in set ratios or percentages), (c) systematically collected and analyzed, and (d) used by the team to determine progress and next steps.

- **Achievable** – While it would be ideal that the youth demonstrate mastery of skills one hundred percent of the time, it is important to take individualized needs into account when creating goals. For example, if a youth currently demonstrates a desired skill twelve percent of the time in a particular setting, they may not be able to reach the goal of demonstrating this skill one hundred percent of the time within a specified time frame. Therefore, an initial goal may be that the youth demonstrate this skill forty percent of the time within the stated amount of time. Meeting the youth where they presently are is a key factor in treatment success.

- **Reliable** – To ensure accuracy and reliability of data collection, treatment providers must account for (a) confounding variables, or any outlying conditions or factors that may skew data, and (b) inconsistencies that may skew data. To mitigate inconsistencies, treatment providers should include in their plan a solid procedure for who will collect data, when, where, and how they will do so.

- **Timely** – When creating and maintaining a treatment plan, time frames in which (a) goals will be achieved and (b) data will be collected, should be taken into consideration. The amount of time given to achieve a specific goal should be individualized to match the needs and abilities of the youth in question. Additionally, the data that will be collected to determine progress should be collected frequently and methodically in order to accurately gage progress and put in place additional supports if needed.

Once purposeful and concrete goals have been established, treatment providers may collect formative data throughout the duration of the time frame allocated for each goal to determine progress, and then summative data at the end of the designated time (with continuous monitoring thereafter). This data will assist in determining any possible regression, how to build upon previously mastered skills, and how to move forward in supporting the youth.

Summary

It is important that treatment providers consider collecting data from multiple settings and contexts in order to gain a well-rounded understanding of the whole youth. From this information, as well as the information presented in previous chapters, treatment providers can fully understand needs and establish specific, actionable goals. Just as important is the synergy and flow of the treatment team. Treatment providers can guide the team by establishing effective collaborative habits and healthy means to resolve any conflict or disagreements. Their commitment, communication, and guidance will lead to the establishment of a productive team and a strong treatment plan that fully aligns with individualized needs.

>>> **QUICK RECAP**

Data Collection:

➢ Multimodal means of data collection from home, school, community, and professional settings should be factored in.

➢ Data collection should be formative, summative, ongoing, and should drive next steps.

➢ Commitment and communication of treatment providers must be consistent, clear, and progressive.

➢ Effective collaborative habits should be established from the get-go. These include:

- Alignment
- Communication
- Collaborative behaviors
- Forging bonds

➢ Conflict resolution should be a healthy part of the collaborative process. Key pieces to remember when disputes arise include:

- Immediate articulation of disputes or disagreements
- Create a healthy system for conflict resolution and respectful mediation
- Model healthy disagreements
- Focus on the issue, not on individuals
- Move forward and check in to ensure full resolution

➢ S.M.A.R.T. Goals – specific, measurable, achievable, reliable, and timely.

Chapter 4

Social Skills and Mental Health Disorders

Boys Town believes that social skill instruction is an integral element in the successful treatment of youth with mental health and/or behavioral disorders. This belief is based on extensive experience, successful treatment outcomes, and comprehensive research that shows that children and adolescents who struggle with emotional, behavioral, and social problems do get better when they learn prosocial skills.

This chapter provides an overview of the effectiveness of social skill instruction in the Boys Town Model, specific outcomes of this skill-based treatment approach in Boys Town's programs, and rationales for providing deliberate social skills training to youth. We also examine how DSM-5 diagnoses can help determine which social skills to target for teaching and what goals to set for treatment.

Social Skill Deficits and the Link to Mental Health Disorders

Studies have demonstrated a link between mental health disorders and social skill deficits. Youth with certain mental health disorders, such as ASD, PTSD, bipolar disorder, anxieties, and ADHD to name a few, tend to lack in social skills as a result of symptoms related to their diagnosis. As a result, youth struggle even further with adaptive living, as well as with overall psychological, academic, and behavioral functioning (Goldstein & DeVries, 2017). These difficulties then extend into adulthood if left untreated.

Researchers have found that, if left without proper training, youth with social skills deficits use maladaptive and unhealthy behaviors that negatively impact their overall health and well-being (Durlak et al., 2011; Ozbay et al., 2007). Evidence can be found in reading a number of state education *Report Cards* and reports, as the data generally shows a trend in behavior/discipline referrals are much more prevalent in youth with mental health concerns when compared to their counterparts. For example, the 2019 Washington State Report Card indicated that students with mental health disorders were disciplined about 2.5 times more than their non-diagnosed or disabled peers (WIRP, 2021). The 2019 Maryland Report Card indicated that students with disabilities represented twenty-seven percent of discipline referrals although they only made up twelve percent of the student population in the state. The cycle of maladaptive social mechanisms adopted by youth with mental health disorders is evident across the nation. This cycle is comprised of the following: mental health symptoms lead to poor social skills, poor social skills then lead to exacerbated concerns or comorbidities, and finally, the two elements intertwine and expand to create a spiral of unhealthy mental and physical conditions (Deighton et al., 2021; Ozbay et al., 2007). If, however, the cycle was broken via proper and effective social skills intervention, youth would gain the healthy interpersonal and intrapersonal competencies needed to find freedom from the cycle and flourish. Moreover, some studies suggest that social skills training may even improve mental health in diagnosed youth, as they gain confidence, peer acceptance, resilience, nourishing friendships, and healthy coping mechanisms (Ratcliffe et al., 2015).

This link between mental health disorders and social skills deficits illustrates the need for focused social skills training for youth with a diagnosis. Adequate social skills are a strong predictor of current and future success in youth. Positive social connections, prosocial behaviors, and adequate social competence are associated with higher levels of happiness, success, positive self-regard, and less stress and worry throughout youth and into adulthood (Andrade et al., 2014; Rubin et al., 2004). In addition, extensive research has found that youth who participate in social skills training have a significant increase in their confidence, academic and test performance, prosocial behaviors, and have reduced behavioral issues and emotional distress as a result of this training (Durlak et al., 2011; Payton et al., 2008). Further research suggests that social skills training can affect central executive cognitive functions as well (Durlak et al., 2011). Research also indicates a correlation between strong social skills and academic achievement, career success, healthy relationships, and positive outlook and well-being (Durlak et al., 2011; Goldstein & DeVries, 2017). Youth who have the social skill set that leads to strong socialization and support tend to demonstrate enduring mental health into adulthood (Goldstein & DeVries, 2017; Schaefer et al., 2017).

Considerations When Determining Social Skill Goals and Approaches for Youth with Mental Health Disorders

Individual needs and experiences are important factors to consider when determining social skill goals. As stated earlier, treatment providers must consider the youth as whole, including developmental, cultural, behavioral, emotional, social, genetic and biological, and various other systems and spheres of influence. In the coming sections, we highlight other core determinants in individualized plan development. These determinants include:

- Externalizing versus internalizing conditions and the possible implications

- Specific mental health disorders and possible corresponding symptoms

- Skills deficits and performance deficits

- Social skill domains

- Possible obstructions to avoid when treatment planning

Externalizing Versus Internalizing Factors and Specific Mental Health Disorders

Understanding specific diagnoses and their underlying conditions is integral in the foundational stages of treatment planning and in determining how to progress throughout implementation. One element of diagnosis to first consider is that of externalizing versus internalizing diagnoses. When a treatment provider is aware of the category in which a specific diagnosis falls, they are better able to determine possible needs as well as treatment approaches to meet those needs. To illustrate, internalizing conditions generally require a different approach to social skills training than externalizing conditions. Youth with externalizing conditions are more likely to display improper and dysregulated behaviors, show aggression, be referred to special services in school, and be more socially isolated due to disruptive conduct. Additionally, research suggests that youth with externalizing disorders tend to function at a lower academic, cognitive, and social level than those with internalizing disorders (McConaughy & Skiba, 1993). Those with internalizing conditions may display less pronounced behaviors, such as withdrawal, passiveness, subjection to bullying behavior, anxiousness and depressive behaviors, and impaired social initiative (Huber, Plötner, & Schmitz, 2019).

Occasionally, you may come across a youth with both externalizing and internalizing conditions. In this case, both categories of need must be addressed. For example, consider a youth who has been diagnosed with both conduct disorder and depression. While it may make sense to some to ensure the primary goals are based on the externalizing behaviors related to conduct disorder, as these behaviors are easier to see, neglecting to treat the depressive symptoms as they impact socialization could result in subpar outcomes and continued internalizing social skill deficits. Comorbid conditions require carefully balanced treatment planning and expertise.

Additionally, certain diagnoses tend to bring with them specific symptoms that impact social skills in a particular manner. For example, a youth with ADHD, hyperactive type, may have difficulty with distractibility and impulsivity which could impact their ability to actively listen, maintain a reciprocal conversation, or maintain socially acceptable and inhibited behaviors. A youth diagnosed with a conduct disorder may struggle with disagreements, expectations, or collaborative efforts with diverse personalities. Meanwhile, a youth diagnosed with Autism Spectrum Disorder may struggle with initiating conversation, staying on topic during non-preferred themes, maintaining eye contact, or recognizing social cues. Understanding the nuances of specific diagnoses offers a strong starting point for determining foundational goals in treatment planning.

Social Skill Deficits Versus Performance Deficits

Before we review the effective outcomes of social skill teaching, it is important to understand why youth need to learn these skills as part of their treatment. Young people require intervention and treatment for many reasons. In this section, we highlight two of the most prevalent: skill deficits and performance deficits. According to Boys Town's philosophy, the development of behavioral and mental health problems in youth can often be linked to youth not learning the social skills needed to overcome problems. In other words, these youth have a "skill deficit", also known as "acquisition deficit," because they have not yet been taught a group of skills, have received inadequate instruction, or have received improper instruction in a particular set of skills. If a youngster has been properly taught and has mastered a skill or set of skills, yet fails to demonstrate the healthy and appropriate behaviors learned, this could indicate a "performance deficit." In the case of a performance deficit, a youth has been taught a skill and has mastered it but there is some underlying component that hinders their ability or desire to demonstrate proficiency. A "fluency deficit," which is closely related to performance deficit, occurs when the youth has not received adequate practice or feedback for the desired skill (NASP, 2017). It is important to distinguish the type of deficit occurring in a youth, as this determines the intervention used. For example, if it is determined that a youth has a skill deficit, then the intervention would focus on foundational instruction and skill acquisition. If it is determined that a "performance deficit" or fluency deficit is at play, then the intervention would focus more on building upon the current skill and removing any hindrances.

Here are two examples of youth with skill deficits:

Kim is a teenager whose mother, Tonya, is the sole caregiver for Kim and her three siblings. Tonya works two jobs to support and provide for her children. She is rarely home, so she usually doesn't have time to prepare home-cooked meals or to eat with her children. Kim, the oldest child, is in charge of feeding her younger siblings. Most days, they eat junk food like potato chips and candy for meals and snacks throughout the night. Kim might occasionally heat up frozen foods or canned goods, which the children eat with their hands in front of the television. Kim is often overwhelmed by the premature responsibility of caring for her siblings. Sometimes, at night, she sneaks bags of potato chips or a pint or two of ice cream out of the kitchen to eat as a way to relax and find a sense of contentment. Since Kim hasn't been taught healthy eating habits or skills related to controlling her eating, and has had no opportunity to learn and develop these skills, she has a skill deficit in the area of "Controlling Eating Habits."

Tariq, a six-year-old boy, always demands candy while waiting in the checkout line with his mother at the grocery store. Usually, Tariq's mother tells him "No." When Tariq hears this answer, he immediately begins to scream and cry, creating quite a scene. Even though Tariq's mother has talked to him about his negative response, he never accepts "No" for an answer. Tariq's mother often gives in and buys him the candy he wants because she's embarrassed and simply wants Tariq to calm down and be quiet. In this situation, Tariq has failed to acquire the social skill of "Accepting 'No' for an Answer" because his mother has not properly taught it to him.

As for performance deficits, a multitude of reasons could factor into why youth don't display skills they have learned. Some reasons proposed by Bellini (2006) include lack of motivation, sensory sensitivities, anxiety, attention problems, impulsivity, memory problems, self-efficacy deficits, and movement or motor issues. In order to determine the factors that could be contributing to a youth's performance deficits, treatment providers could consider various means such as observations, interviews, or a FBA. A focused and individualized intervention can be accomplished once the contributing factor or factors are established, as they shed light on missing pieces and how to fill gaps.

Let's look at an example of a performance deficit that results from lack of motivation. In this situation, the youth is not internally motivated to use a skill so an external reward the youth values must be implemented.

Josh is a competent student who usually does well on tests. Currently, however, he is failing several classes because he is not completing his homework. Grades aren't a big deal to Josh. He isn't internally motivated to earn A's, and he doesn't see any payoff for getting them. Josh is fully capable of completing his homework; he sometimes does it when it's raining outside just so he has something to do. In this situation, Josh can perform the skill of "Completing Homework" but chooses not to. One way to address this is to set up a contingency where Josh can't go outside to play with his friends until he completes his homework. Most likely, Josh will begin to use the skill because he now has an external motivation (going outside to play) to perform the skill correctly.

The best way treatment providers can differentiate between a skill deficit and a performance deficit is to ask five questions identified by Bellini (2006, p. 115) during the assessment of a youth.

1. Does the child perform the skill across multiple settings and persons?

2. Does the child perform the skill without support or assistance?

3. Does the child perform the skill fluently and effortlessly?

4. Does the child perform the skill when reinforcement is provided?

5. Does the child perform the skill when environmental modifications are made?"

If the answer to most of these questions is "Yes" during an assessment, it is likely the youth has a performance deficit rather than a skill deficit. If the answer to most of the questions is "No," the youth probably has a skill deficit.

Finally, skill deficits and performance deficits are not always exclusive. It is possible for a youth to not fully acquire a skill and not have the motivation to develop and use it. In these cases, both skill training and an intervention that addresses performance (e.g., motivation system, self-monitoring intervention) are necessary to target combined deficit issues. (The Boys Town Model addresses both deficit forms by combining social skill training with a token economy.)

Social Skills Domains

According to Dr. Howard Knoff's "Stop and Think" social skills program and the National Association of School Psychologists (NASP), four domains that social skills can be broken down into include:

- *survival,* such as following directives that promote a positive environment, ignoring distractions, and other skills that are conducive to learning and performing to standard

- *interpersonal,* such as collaborative skills, good sportsmanship, and skills related to healthy conversation maintenance

- *problem-solving,* such as decision-making, genuinely apologizing, and asking for help

- *conflict resolution,* such as dealing with peer pressure, bullying, and other social dilemmas in a healthy manner

Another model, coined the Social Thinking Model by Michelle Garcia-Winner (2019), describes other paramount social competencies that may be considered when treatment planning. These competencies include: self-regulation, social-emotional learning, executive functioning, perspective taking, and social problem-solving. Foundational areas of focus, according to Garcia-Winner's model, include:

- *social attention,* or awareness and interpretation of settings, social contexts, and social situations

- *social interpretation,* or understanding context in terms of self and others, intentions, and information surrounding social experiences

- *social problem-solving,* or using information to determine a social need or happening, goals, and how to respond accordingly

And from these three areas comes:

- *social response,* or evaluation of self, the situation, practicing cognitive self-regulation, and bringing every social competency together in order to respond in a healthy and productive manner

When creating an individualized treatment plan, treatment providers may choose to lean towards these domains and components as foundational areas of focus. While there are hundreds of social skills to consider, honing in on specific domains in order to gain a holistic birds-eye view of individualized needs in specific areas may help in the initial planning stages.

Possible Obstructions to Avoid in Social Skills Treatment Planning and Implementation

Studies have shown that purposeful and thoughtful execution of social skills training leads to greater success in achieving desired outcomes and reaching goals in a manner that extends beyond the time frame of training and beyond the scope of training context. We have explored the importance of *collaboration, communication, buy-in, parental/caregiver involvement,* and *understanding the specific needs of the youth* in regards to their unique composition when planning treatment. Now, let's focus on other components that maximize the quality and value of individualized social skills training, including obstructions to avoid and effective treatment techniques.

Invention choice is a fundamental attribute to effective treatment planning (Goldstein & DeVries, 2017). The number of social skills programs available today are as countless as the individual pixels that come together to create each unique youth and as broad as the needs that they were created to serve. Some interventions focus too narrowly on one or few concrete topics, neglecting social competence as a whole and the multiple layers that lead to overarching success for youth with specific layered needs. Others have a focus that may be too exhaustive, touching on the multiple layers of social competence but in a superficial and rushed manner that may be inadequate for youth who require intensive, sustained, and methodical training. Treatment providers should therefore choose evidence-based and data-driven interventions that best align with individual needs (broad versus narrow skill attainment, approaches to training, diagnosis-specific, adequate duration, etc.).

Variation of the environment in which social skills training takes place could be another aspect of successful training implementation. When placed in a controlled environment where expectations are clear and context is predictable, we all most likely will perform better and achieve at a higher degree than when asked to perform the same task and behaviors in less controlled and more organic situations. Consistent training in such a setting can obstruct the impact of treatment. In contrast, providing ample opportunity to safely practice skills in a variety of settings and more natural and diverse environments will enhance confidence, ability, and overall gain in skill set. This also is another area where parent/caregiver involvement can prove to be game changing, as practice in the home and out in the community will naturally increase success.

Practicality of social skills that transfer into everyday life is yet another consideration when planning treatment goals and intervention implementation (Goldstein & DeVries, 2017). As treatment providers analyze needs and determine targeted skills and competencies, social skills program choice, and training technique, they should also be cognizant of skill functionality and application. In other words, treatment providers should ask: Are these skills and the manner in which they are delivered generalizable? Are they adaptable and applicable in multiple social scenarios? Do they lend themselves to other social competencies? Addressing these questions may optimize treatment.

Addressing cognitive and affective factors is another component that is essential to quality social skills intervention, according to Goldstein & DeVries (2017). Cognitive factors, such as memory, attention, or distorted thinking patterns, may impact a youth's perspective and ability to process new information in a realistic and constructive way. Affective factors, such as emotional regulation, motivation, and attitude could also potentially undermine information processing and ability or desire to apply new social skills knowledge. Therefore, it is important to recognize these potential impediments and address them accordingly in conjunction with social skills training.

Keeping the objective of social competence at the forefront is a final factor in delivering quality social skill instruction. This means taking into account a youth's emotional functioning, as well as the social context, such as the personalized considerations reviewed earlier in this book, function/intentions of the interaction, relationship with the intended recipient/recipients of communication, and time (Semrud-Clikeman, 2007;

Spitzberg, 2003). Additionally, treatment providers would benefit from viewing social skills as building blocks which reinforce the larger structure of social competency when combined with social and interpersonal communication (Semrud-Clikeman, 2007). Each of these components of social competence are goal-oriented, involve correct situational perceptions, and involve situational interactions that align with the situation (Semrud-Clikeman, 2007). The components of social communication and interpersonal communication, however, require social skills training to be properly executed.

In addition to the previous considerations, implementation of social skills training should include a variety of techniques. Some evidence-based approaches include: role-play, modeling and rehearsal, games, use of technology (videos, games, apps, etc.), and self-monitoring and data tracking (Durlak et al., 2011; Goldstein & DeVries, 2017). Additionally, treatment providers should ensure possible obstructions at home/with caregivers and core support systems are minimized. For example, treatment providers could...

- provide clear, concrete, and undemanding methods for extending social skills training into common outside settings.

- share ideas for experiential practice at home, around town, or when participating in team or group activities.

- offer open conversations and tips for caregivers on how they can avoid letting their own emotions take over and acting on impulse in moments of frustration.

- provide premade, fluid, and editable documents, trackers, visuals, and charts for use in outside settings.

- provide other resources such as books, trainings, online resources, parent groups, and listservs.

- provide conversation starters or ideas for how to respond to the youth, *should* the youth have questions about their diagnosis, about the treatment plan, about their needs in comparison to peers or siblings, etc.

Attention to the data, to possible obstructions that arise, and to multimodal training implementation are surefire ways to ensure highly beneficial treatment outcomes.

Social Skill Instruction and the Boys Town Model

The overall goal of the Boys Town Model is to help youth learn how to become productive adults who can make good decisions, interact positively with others in society, and find success in their lives. Two of the Model's hallmarks are teaching social skills and learning how to build positive relationships, both of which result in intrinsic changes within youth. Social skills taught through the Model are very important for youngsters because they provide the foundation upon which many other more complex and advanced skills can be built. Acquiring these "keystone" self-help skills opens up a myriad of possibilities for change – emotionally, behaviorally, and socially – that otherwise might not have been present.

By learning self-help skills, children can change the way they think, feel, and act. This is a learning process. Boys Town's teaching methods utilize behavioral principles while allowing children to integrate their thoughts and feelings into this learning process. Boys Town also uses external reinforcement, when appropriate, to promote and maintain skill-learning and relationship development. As changes in external behavior occur, internal shifts also occur. These enable youth to change intrinsically. Inadequate thought patterns are reframed, negative feelings diminish, and inappropriate behaviors are replaced by positive behaviors, which benefit both the youth and those who interact with them.

As we stress the importance and benefits of social skill instruction for youth with mental health disorders, it is imperative for treatment providers to understand that the success youth achieve in Boys Town programs results not only from learning social skills but from a complete and comprehensive treatment environment.

Youth in Boys Town programs – especially those in long-term residential settings – live and learn in a highly structured environment where therapeutic treatment is a part of everything they do. The positive outcomes of youth treatment involving social skill instruction that are presented later in this chapter must be understood in the context of a larger treatment approach. (For a more detailed description of the role social skill instruction plays in the Boys Town Model, see *Teaching Social Skills to Youth: An easy-to-follow guide to teaching 196 basic to complex life skills, fourth edition,* by Jeff Tierney and Erin Green, published by Boys Town Press.)

Fundamentals of Skill-Based Treatment

The environments of troubled youth who require treatment significantly contribute to and foster the formation of their problem behaviors and mental health difficulties. However, these learned inappropriate behaviors and skills serve a purpose. They enable youth to get what they need and want and/or avoid something they don't like or don't want. Over time, these same behaviors and skills become reinforced and strengthened, and eventually spill over into other environments (school, extracurricular activities, jobs, relationships with peers and adults, and so on).

When youth with strong learning histories that support negative behavior encounter new environments or settings, they typically use the same negative behaviors that were successful for them in the past. When these behaviors don't work, kids flounder, unsure of what it takes to be successful. For youth to succeed in familiar and unfamiliar environments, situations, and relationships, they must learn new prosocial skills that will help them get their needs and wants met in ways that are more socially acceptable. This is the aim of the Boys Town Model and the role of social skill instruction.

Boys Town's social skill instruction approach to treatment focuses on teaching the essential life skills young people need in order to make the successful transition into young adulthood (Peter, 1999). Social, academic, and vocational skills, as well as spiritual values, are taught in a "family-style" treatment setting through proactively teaching at neutral times, reinforcing positive behavior as it occurs, practicing and rehearsing, correcting inappropriate behavior in a positive style, and helping youth learn to use alternative appropriate behaviors when they face crisis situations.

According to Gresham (1998), a social skill is defined as "socially acceptable learned behaviors enabling the individual to interact effectively with others and avoid or escape socially unacceptable behavior exhibited by others" (p.20). Thus, social skills enable youth to appropriately and effectively behave in the various environments they inhabit (home, school, work, etc.). These skills not only produce positive consequences for the individual but also are socially acceptable and responsive to others.

With social skill instruction, youth learn skills that are determined to be the most functional for them and expected to produce the best long-term results. This means that every youth requires individual treatment. As explained in Chapter 2, some youth will initially need to learn the most basic skills ("Following Instructions," "Accepting Consequences," "Accepting 'No' for an Answer," etc.) in order to lay a foundation for more complex skills ("Expressing Feelings Appropriately," "Resisting Peer Pressure," "Using Spontaneous Problem-Solving," etc.). Many times, treatment providers will need to gradually shape a youth's behavior by patiently teaching basic social skills so that the youth can learn the final desired behavior. This can be a slow, arduous process for treatment providers and youth, but it is necessary if the youth is to overcome their problems. (Eight basic social skills and their steps are provided in the Appendix.)

The use of appropriate social skills involves an immensely complex chain of rapidly occurring interpersonal events. For youth, especially those suffering from mental health disorders that dramatically limit their emotional and behavioral functioning, correctly performing these skills at the right time can be an overwhelming task. They may have considerable difficulty organizing and blending their behaviors into smooth flowing interactions with others, particularly under stressful conditions. So, treatment providers must be able and willing to adjust their teaching techniques, vocabulary, and interpersonal behaviors to best meet the learning style of each youth in their care.

When choosing social skills for treatment, it is important for providers to take into account individual factors like the age and developmental level of the youth, severity of the youth's behaviors, the length of time a youth has been exposed to social skill instruction, and other factors outlined in Chapter 2. Individual considerations play a pivotal role in the success or failure of each youth's treatment plan. Once the most appropriate skills have been identified and prioritized, treatment providers can utilize the various teaching interactions developed at Boys Town to reinforce and teach youth new, prosocial ways of getting their needs met.

The Boys Town Social Skills Curriculum contains 196 skills that address a wide variety of youth issues at all levels, from minor school- or home-related problems to skill deficits associated with more serious problems like aggression, delinquency, and depression. All 196 curriculum skills, the steps to each skill, and the teaching interactions that form the cornerstone of treatment planning and active intervention at Boys Town are presented in Boys Town's book, *Teaching Social Skills to Youth: An easy-to-follow guide to teaching 196 basic to complex life skills, fourth edition.* The Social Skills Curriculum and teaching techniques described in that book can be easily integrated into a variety of settings (natural home environment, foster home, emergency shelter care program, group home residential program, psychiatric treatment program, and many others).

A Proven, Effective Treatment Strategy

How do we know that social skill instruction – one of the hallmarks of the Boys Town Model – is a therapeutic, effective treatment strategy? For starters, the Boys Town Model grew out of behavioral research conducted by Montrose Wolf, one of the pioneers in the applied behavior analysis movement. In the late 1960s and early 1970s, Wolf and his colleagues began their research to design a new treatment model for troubled youth as an effective alternative to the standard state-run programs of the time. The new model came to be known as the Teaching-Family Model, and it was adopted by Boys Town in 1975 (Risley, 2005). The Teaching-Family Model has been tested time and time again, across numerous settings and behavior problems, with positive results (Fixsen, Blasé, Timbers, & Wolf, 2001).

The Teaching-Family Model combines multiple components including a token-economy motivation system, detailed specification and monitoring of the desired behaviors, and skill teaching of desired behaviors. All this takes place within a family home setting where the primary "teachers" or "house parents" are a married couple (Wolf, Kirigin, Fixen, Blasé, & Braukmann, 1995). The Boys Town Model, which is used in all Boys Town programs, utilizes the components previously listed, with a specific focus on teaching social skills.

While youth are treated at Boys Town, a variety of data is gathered. Standardized outcome instruments like those highlighted in Chapter 1 (CBCL, DISC, etc.) are frequently administered to youth. Improvements on these instruments often occur because youth learn and successfully use the social skills that are taught as part of their treatment. For example, an examination of the admission and departure Child Behavior Checklist (CBCL) scores for youth who left the Boys Town Family Home Program® between 2001 and 2004 revealed that eighty percent of the girls and sixty-three percent of the boys were admitted with a CBCL total score in the clinically significant range. Remarkably, these scores had dropped to twenty-five percent for girls and twenty-four percent for boys by the time these youth departed the program (Figure 1).

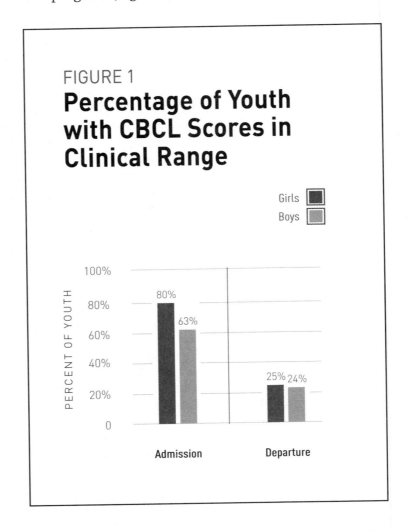

FIGURE 1

Percentage of Youth with CBCL Scores in Clinical Range

Girls
Boys

Further, youth admitted during this same time frame arrived with a variety of mental health issues that improved significantly during treatment. For example, seventy-two percent of girls and fifty-four percent of boys were admitted with a DSM diagnosis. Twelve months later, only thirty percent of girls and twenty-four percent of boys continued to meet criteria for a formal DSM diagnosis (Figure 2) (Boys Town National Research Institute for Child and Family Studies, 2006a).

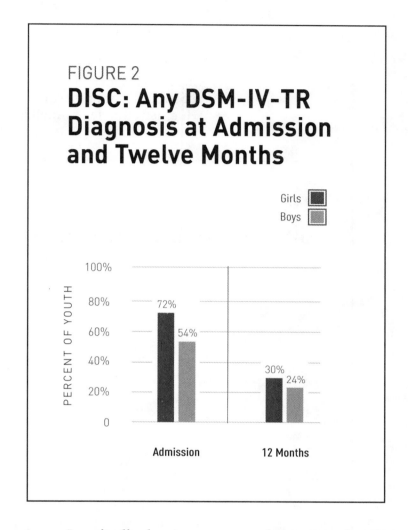

FIGURE 2

DISC: Any DSM-IV-TR Diagnosis at Admission and Twelve Months

Longitudinal outcome research suggests that the effects of treatment at Boys Town continue after youth depart from the program. One such study, an extensive sixteen-year follow-up completed in 2003, involved 211 former Boys Town youth and forty-one "comparison" youth who were accepted for admission to Boys Town but never came. Participants, ages twenty-seven to thirty-seven, completed a 151-item survey measuring several life domains. Results produced two major findings: 1) As adults, those participants who received treatment at Boys Town were more likely to be functioning as productive, law-abiding citizens than those who did not, and 2) the longer these former Boys Town youth were in the treatment program, the more positive the long-term outcomes. For example, when looking at criminality, the youth who received eighteen months or more of treatment at Boys Town had lower rates of incarceration, recent arrests, criminal activity, and Intimate Partner Violence (IPV) than those youth who received six months of treatment or less (Figure 3) (Huefner, Ringle, Chmelka, & Ingram, 2007; Ringle, Chmelka, Ingram, & Huefner, 2006).

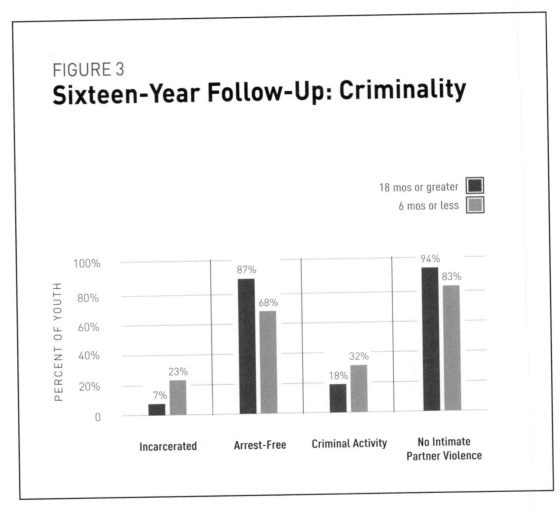

FIGURE 3

Sixteen-Year Follow-Up: Criminality

In 2006, the Boys Town National Research Institute completed a five-year follow-up study of Boys Town youth who departed in the year 2000. Approximately two hundred former Boys Town youth (with an average age of twenty-one) responded to an eighty-five-item survey that measured social functioning and quality of life across a variety of domains. These youth entered care with a variety of risk factors, including school problems, being out-of-parental control, aggression, depression, substance use, and interpersonal problems. Five years after leaving treatment, the former Boys Town youth were functioning similar to their peers in the general population in areas like education, employment, and overall positive mental health (Figure 4). These outcomes provide strong evidence of the efficacy of the Boys Town Model in teaching lasting social skills to youth who are struggling within everyday society (Thompson, Ringle, & Kingsley, 2007; Boys Town National Research Institute for Child and Family Studies, 2006b; Kingsley et al., 2008).

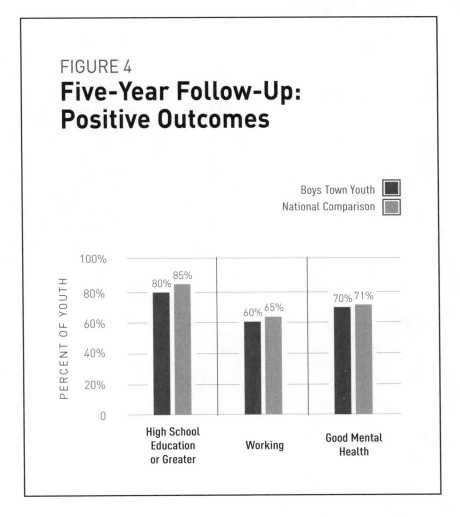

FIGURE 4

Five-Year Follow-Up: Positive Outcomes

We believe all the research presented here, as well as numerous other positive findings (e.g., Handwerk et al., 2008; Larzelere, Daly, Davis, Chmelka, & Handwerk,

2004; Thompson et al., 1996), verify that the Boys Town Model, with its emphasis on social skill training, is an effective, therapeutic treatment option. Just as other strategies (psychotropic medication; individual, family, or group therapy; and behavioral interventions) are prescribed as part of a youth's treatment plan, so too are the specific social skills that youth need to learn. Once youth have mastered these skills, they are better able to appropriately and effectively interact with their environment and those in it.

Summary

The core of the Boys Town Model involves teaching youth social skills and how to build relationships. The Model incorporates a social skill instruction approach – teaching youth positive alternative skills that can replace negative behaviors – while also recognizing the importance and need for other types of treatment strategies like medications and therapy, as important ingredients to an overall treatment plan. Equally important to successful treatment planning are prescribing and assigning suitable social skills for targeted teaching by treatment providers. Boys Town's extensive research has shown that social skill instruction, in a wide variety of treatment settings, is a valuable and effective treatment option for helping troubled youth overcome their problems.

 **QUICK RECAP**

Social Skills Deficits and Mental Health Disorders:

- Research suggests a link between social skill deficits and mental health disorders, as symptoms of diagnoses can impede social competence.

- Maladaptive coping strategies of social skills deficits can extend into adulthood, impacting psychological, academic, and behavioral functioning if left untreated.

- Studies show that social skills training increases youth confidence, academic performance, prosocial behaviors, and emotional wellness.

Considerations in Treatment Planning for Youth with Mental Health Disorders:

- Externalizing versus internalizing conditions and the possible implications, such as aggressive, impulsive, or acting out behaviors versus withdrawal, isolation, and anxiety.

- Specific mental health disorders and possible corresponding symptoms, such as symptom differences between a youth diagnosed with ADHD as opposed to a youth diagnosed with ASD.

- Skills deficits and performance deficits, or rather a lack of training versus inconsistent or failure to consistently demonstrate a previously taught skill.

- Social skill domains, such as Knoff's "Stop and Think" domains of survival, interpersonal, problem-solving and conflict-resolution, or Garcia-Winner's "Social Thinking Model" areas of social attention, social interpretation, and social problem-solving leading to social response.

(Cont.)

➤ Possible obstructions to avoid when treatment planning:

- Misaligned intervention choice

- Singular and/or unnatural treatment settings/environment

- Not addressing individual cognitive and affective factors

- Teaching impractical social skills that cannot be translated into the outside world

- Forgetting the end goal or getting caught up in smaller details

- Limited variety of treatment approaches and/or method choices that do not suit the specific youth

- Discrepancies or incontinuities between the institution where treatment takes place and the home or other core settings

Boys Town Model:

➤ Two hallmarks of this comprehensive Model, (1) teaching social skills, and (2) learning how to build positive relationships, result in intrinsic changes within youth.

➤ Provides "keystone" self-help skills that act as building blocks in strengthening long-term overall social, emotional, and psychological well-being.

➤ Research studies conducted on the Boys Town Model have produced hopeful outcomes including:

- Adults who participated in the Boys Town Model in childhood were more likely to lead more productive and positive lives.

- Longer participation in the Boys Town program led to more positive long-term outcomes.

Chapter 5

Social Skill Charts for Specific Mental Health Disorders

The charts presented in this chapter are helpful guides for including social skill instruction in individualized treatment plans for youth with mental health disorders. Treatment teams that use these charts can more easily and efficiently identify and prescribe social skills that are appropriate for a specific DSM-5 diagnosis and individually suited to meet each child's treatment goals.

The charts are arranged by the order and sections used in the DSM-5. The diagnoses and social skills covered in the charts were selected by a panel of youthcare experts at Boys Town. Not all diagnoses or sections from the DSM-5 are listed because some diagnoses do not readily lend themselves to social skill instruction or are not commonly diagnosed in children and adolescents.

For each DSM-5 diagnosis, there is a list of suggested social skills. In some cases, the skills are combined for several disorders within a section that may be associated with similar skill deficits. Suggested social skills are ones treatment providers can target and teach to youth who have a particular disorder and are lacking in certain skill areas. The skills are grouped according to their level of mastery – basic, intermediate, advanced, and complex.

Treatment providers can use the skill lists during the treatment planning process to help determine appropriate goals and objectives for youth with particular mental health disorders. Selections of specific skills should not be based solely on a DSM-5 diagnosis, but rather on specific referral concerns and current problems youth are exhibiting. It is important to remember that treatment planning – including determining which social skills to teach – should be individualized to meet the specific needs of each child. Even when youth are diagnosed with the same disorder, skill deficits or performance deficits will vary, and each youth will display symptoms associated with a diagnosis differently. Usually, a treatment team will choose skills that address a youth's specific deficits and needs and help meet their overall treatment goals. For example, after evaluating two youth who are diagnosed with Post-Traumatic Stress Disorder, the treatment team might recommend teaching the social skill of "Saying 'No' Assertively" for one youth because she relaxed her personal boundaries following her trauma experience. The team then might recommend teaching the social skill of "Participating in Activities" for the second youth because he has been withdrawn since his trauma experience. Ultimately, a youth's individual expression of their diagnosis and particular social skills deficits, as well as individual considerations (developmental, cultural, social, etc.), should guide decisions on what specific skills to target for treatment.

As the treatment planning process for social skills training begins and unfolds, treatment providers can use the appropriate charts to select skills that best fit a youngster's treatment needs. Let's look at an example of how this might work: Carla is a sixteen-year-old who has been diagnosed with Reactive Attachment Disorder. She has been admitted to a residential group home facility because she frequently yells and swears at her adopted parents, doesn't follow instructions at home and school, hangs out with inappropriate friends, and engages in promiscuous activity with multiple male peers.

At the first treatment team meeting, the team determines that the primary goal for Carla will be to build positive relationships with others. Next, the team looks at the social skills listed on the charts for Reactive Attachment Disorder to identify skills to teach Carla that would help her meet this goal and skill deficit objective. After identifying skills and objectives, the team determines how progress is to be monitored for each objective and what level of improvement they expect for each objective before the next team meeting. Throughout the meeting, team members consider Carla's individual characteristics to ensure that the social skills and other components of the treatment plan meet her individual needs.

Since Carla's primary difficulty is with male peers, one skill selected for the goal of building positive relationships is "Setting Appropriate Boundaries." School staff will monitor Carla's progress with this skill since school is the primary setting where Carla interacts with male peers. School staff will record positive and negative interactions with males on a behavior card as they occur. Since Carla has shown she is not able to use the skill of "Setting Appropriate Boundaries," the initial goal is modest; however, expectations will increase as Carla practices the skill and shows progress. The team decides that a three-to-one ratio of positive-to-negative interactions with males is a realistic starting goal. The team uses this same process to select other skills and objectives that fit the goal of building positive relationships with others, and members identify two more goals and social skills from the Reactive Attachment Disorder chart for those goals, based on Carla's current symptoms and history. After the team meeting, Carla's youth care supervisor writes out an individualized treatment plan, which includes the appropriate social skills to be taught, based on the results and conclusions of the treatment team meeting.

A good treatment plan is the first step to effective treatment. When treatment providers use the kind of treatment planning process just outlined, along with the charts that follow, they can better select the social skills that best fit each youth's treatment plans and individual needs.

Categories that May Impact Youth	Diagnosis and Examples Within Each
Neurodevelopmental Disorder	**Intellectual Disabilities:** Intellectual Developmental Disorder, Global Developmental Delay, Unspecified Intellectual Developmental Disorder **Communication Disorders:** Language Disorder, Speech-Sound Disorder, Childhood-Onset Fluency Disorder, Social Communication Disorder, Unspecified Communication Disorder **Autism Spectrum Disorder** Attention-Deficit/Hyperactivity Disorder: AD/HD, Other Specified or Unspecified AD/HD **Specific Learning Disorder** **Motor Disorders:** Developmental Coordination Disorder, Stereotypic Movement Disorder, Tic Disorder, Tourette's Disorder, Persistent Motor or Vocal Tic Disorder, Provisional Tic Disorder, Other Specified or Unspecified Tic Disorder
Schizophrenia Spectrum/ Other Psychotic Disorders *Early onset is rare*	Schizotypal Disorder, Brief Psychotic Disorder, Schizophreniform Disorder, Schizoaffective Disorder, Schizophrenia, Delusional Disorder, Other Specified or Unspecified, Substance or Medical-Induced
Bipolar and Related Disorders	Bipolar I, Bipolar II, Cyclothymic Disorder, Other Specified or Unspecified, Substance or Medical-Induced
Depressive Disorders	Disruptive Mood Dysregulation Disorder, Major Depressive Disorder, Premenstrual Dysphoric Disorder, Catatonia, Due to Another Medical Condition, Other Specified or Unspecified, Substance or Medical-Induced

Categories that May Impact Youth	Diagnosis and Examples Within Each
Anxiety Disorders	Generalized Anxiety Disorder, Separation Anxiety, Selective Mutism, Specific Phobia, Social Anxiety Disorder, Panic Disorder, Panic Attack, Agoraphobia, Due to Another Medical Condition, Other Specified or Unspecified
Obsessive-Compulsive/ Related Disorders	Obsessive-Compulsive Disorder, Body Dysmorphic Disorder, Hoarding Disorder, Trichotillomania, Excoriation Disorder, Other Specified or Unspecified, Substance or Medical-Induced
Trauma/Stressor-Related Disorders	Reactive-Attachment Disorders, Disinhibited Social Engagement Disorders, Post-Traumatic Stress Disorder, Acute Stress Disorder, Adjustment Disorder, Other Specified or Unspecified
Dissociative Disorders	Dissociative Identity Disorder, Dissociative Amnesia, Depersonalization/ Derealization Disorder, Other Specified or Unspecified
Somatic Symptom/ Related Disorders	Somatic Symptom Disorder, Illness Anxiety Disorder, Conversion Disorder, Due to Another Medical Condition, Other Specified or Unspecified
Feeding and Eating Disorders	Pica, Rumination Disorder, Avoidant/Restrictive Food Intake Disorder, Anorexia Nervosa, Bulimia Nervosa, Binge-Eating Disorder, Other Specified or Unspecified
Elimination Disorders	Enuresis, Encopresis, Other Specified or Unspecified
Sleep-Wake Disorders	**Sleep-Wake Disorders:** *Insomnia Disorder, Hypersomnolence Disorder, Narcolepsy* **Breathing-Related Sleep Disorder:** Obstructive Sleep Apnea, Circadian Rhythm Sleep-Wake Disorder **Parasomnia:** *Rapid/Non-Rapid Eye Movement Sleep Behavior Disorder, Sleep Terrors*

Categories that May Impact Youth	Diagnosis and Examples Within Each
Gender Dysphoria	Gender Dysphoria, Other Specified or Unspecified
Disruptive, Impulse-Control, and Conduct Disorders	Oppositional Defiant Disorder, Intermittent Explosive Disorder, Conduct Disorder, Antisocial Personality Disorder, Pyromania, Kleptomania, Other Specified or Unspecified
Substance-Related and Addictive Disorders	**Substance-Related Disorders:** Substance Use, Substance-Induced, Substance Intoxication, Withdrawal, Medical-Related **Alcohol, Caffeine, Cannabis, Hallucinogen, Inhalant, Opioid, Sedative, Hypnotic, Anxiolytic, Stimulant, Tobacco, and Other-Related Disorders:** *Use Disorder, Intoxication, Withdrawal, Other Unspecified*
Personality Disorders	**Personality Disorder:** General Personality Disorder **Cluster A Personality Disorder:** Paranoid Personality Disorder, Schizoid Personality Disorder, Schizotypal Personality Disorder **Cluster B Personality Disorder:** Antisocial Personality, Borderline Personality Disorder, Histrionic Personality Disorder, Narcissistic Personality Disorder **Cluster C Personality Disorder:** Avoidant Personality Disorder, Dependent Personality Disorder, Obsessive-Compulsive Personality Disorder
Other Mental Disorders	Other Specified or Unspecified, Due to other Medical Condition
Other Conditions	Other Conditions, Medical-Induced Movement Disorders
Conditions for Further Study *Not Categories but rather are being researched*	Suicidal Behavior, Non-Suicidal Self Injury, Internet Gaming Disorder, Caffeine Use Disorder

Disorders Usually Diagnosed in Infancy, Childhood, or Adolescence

INTELLECTUAL DISABILITY

Suggested Social Skills Training for Individuals Diagnosed with Mild Intellectual Disabilities

BASIC SKILLS

- Accepting Criticism (Feedback) or a Consequence
- Accepting "No" for an Answer
- Disagreeing Appropriately
- Following Instructions
- Introducing Yourself
- Talking with Others

INTERMEDIATE SKILLS

- Accepting Apologies from Others
- Accepting Compliments
- Accepting Consequences
- Accepting Decisions of Authority
- Agreeing to Disagree
- Answering the Phone
- Asking for Clarification
- Asking for Help
- Asking for Permission
- Asking Questions
- Checking In (or Checking Back)
- Closing a Conversation
- Completing Tasks
- Complying with a Reasonable Request
- Contributing to a Discussion (Joining in a Conversation)

- Giving Compliments
- Greeting Others
- Ignoring Distractions
- Initiating a Conversation
- Interrupting Appropriately
- Introducing Others
- Listening to Others
- Maintaining a Conversation
- Maintaining an Appropriate Appearance
- Making an Apology
- Making a Phone Call
- Making a Request (Asking a Favor)
- Participating in Activities
- Reporting Emergencies
- Reporting Other Youths' Behavior (or Peer Reporting)
- Resisting Peer Pressure
- Responding to Persons of Authority
- Saying Goodbye to Guest
- Saying "No" Assertively
- Seeking Positive Attention
- Sharing Something
- Showing Appreciation
- Staying on Task
- Switching from One Task to Another

Intellectual Disability (Cont.)

- Trying New Tasks
- Using an Appropriate Voice Tone (or Level)
- Using Anger Control Strategies
- Using Table Etiquette
- Waiting Your Turn
- Working with Others

ADVANCED SKILLS

- Accepting Defeat or Loss
- Accepting Help or Assistance
- Accepting Winning Appropriately
- Caring for Others' Property
- Caring for Your Own Belongings
- Choosing Appropriate Clothing
- Choosing Appropriate Friends
- Communicating Honestly
- Concentrating on a Subject or Task
- Contributing to Group Activities
- Controlling Eating Habits
- Coping with Anger and Aggression from Others
- Coping with Change
- Coping with Conflict
- Coping with Sad Feelings (or Depression)
- Dealing with Being Left Out
- Dealing with Boredom
- Dealing with Contradictory Messages
- Dealing with Failure
- Dealing with Fear

- Dealing with Frustration
- Dealing with Group Pressure
- Dealing with Rejection
- Delaying Gratification
- Displaying Effort
- Displaying Sportsmanship
- Expressing Appropriate Affection
- Expressing Feelings Appropriately
- Expressing Pride in Accomplishments
- Following Safety Rules
- Interacting Appropriately with the Opposite Sex
- Keeping Property in Its Place
- Lending to Others
- Making New Friends
- Organizing Tasks and Activities
- Persevering on Tasks and Projects
- Planning Meals
- Preparing for a Stressful Conversation
- Preventing Trouble with Others
- Responding to Others' Humor
- Responding to Teasing
- Self-Reporting Your Own Behaviors
- Setting Appropriate Boundaries
- Sharing Attention with Others
- Sharing Personal Experiences
- Sticking Up for Yourself
- Suggesting an Activity
- Using Appropriate Humor
- Using Appropriate Language

Intellectual Disability (Cont.)

- Using Relaxation Strategies
- Using Self-Talk or Self-Instruction
- Using Study Skills

COMPLEX SKILLS

- Asking for Advice
- Assessing Your Own Abilities
- Being a Consumer
- Being Assertive
- Being Patient
- Budgeting and Managing Money
- Differentiating Friends from Acquaintances
- Displaying Appropriate Control
- Identifying Your Own Feelings
- Interviewing for a Job
- Maintaining Relationships
- Making an Appropriate Complaint
- Planning Ahead
- Recognizing Moods of Others
- Resolving Conflicts
- Seeking Professional Assistance
- Using Community Resources
- Using Leisure Time
- Using Strategies to Find a Job

COMMUNICATION DISORDERS

Language Disorder
Speech-Sound Disorder
Child-Onset Fluency Disorder
Social Communication Disorder
Unspecified Communication Disorder

Suggested Social Skills Training for Individuals Diagnosed with a Communication Disorder

BASIC SKILLS

- Introducing Yourself
- Returning Friendly Greetings
- Talking with Others
- Using an Appropriate Voice Tone (or Level)
- Using Appropriate Gestures

INTERMEDIATE SKILLS

- Agreeing to Disagree
- Asking for Clarification
- Asking for Help
- Asking for Permission
- Asking Questions
- Choosing Appropriate Words
- Closing a Conversation
- Cooperating with Peers
- Getting Another Person's Attention
- Getting the Teacher's Attention
- Giving and Accepting Compliments
- Greeting Others with Appropriate Verbal and Nonverbal Language
- Initiating a Conversation
- Introducing Others
- Maintaining Appropriate Pace in Conversation

- Participating in Reciprocal Play
- Recognizing, Responding to, and Conveying Feelings Through Nonverbal Communication
- Responding to Persons of Authority
- Saying "No" Assertively
- Sharing Something
- Showing Appreciation
- Showing Interest
- Staying on Topic
- Sticking Up for Others
- Sticking Up for Yourself
- Using Conversation Maintenance Strategies
- Using Helpful Language and Assisting Peers
- Working with Others

ADVANCED SKILLS

- Adjusting Behavior Based on Social Cues
- Analyzing Skills Needed for Different Situations
- Analyzing Social Situations
- Contributing to Group Activities
- Expressing Feelings Appropriately

Communication Disorders (Cont.)

- Gaining Consent
- Giving Consent
- Giving Rationales
- Making and Keeping Friends
- Responding to Others' Feelings
- Responding to Others' Humor
- Understanding Figurative Language
- Using Communication Breakdown Strategies to Improve Intelligibility
- Using Self-Talk or Self-Instruction

COMPLEX SKILLS

- Accurately Identifying the Perspective of Others
- Being Assertive
- Setting Goals
- Taking Risks Appropriately
- Using Problem-Solving Strategies
- Using Self-Monitoring and Self-Reflection

AUTISM SPECTRUM DISORDER

Suggested Social Skills Training for Individuals Diagnosed with Autism Spectrum Disorder

BASIC SKILLS

- Accepting Criticism (Feedback) or a Consequence
- Accepting "No" for an Answer
- Disagreeing Appropriately
- Following Instructions
- Introducing Yourself
- Showing Respect
- Showing Sensitivity to Others
- Talking with Others

INTERMEDIATE SKILLS

- Accepting Apologies from Others
- Accepting Compliments
- Accepting Consequences
- Accepting Decisions of Authority
- Agreeing to Disagree
- Answering the Phone
- Asking for Clarification
- Asking for Help
- Asking for Permission
- Asking for Time to Cool Down
- Asking Questions
- Checking In (or Checking Back)
- Choosing Appropriate Words
- Closing a Conversation
- Complying with a Reasonable Request
- Contributing to a Discussion (Joining in a Conversation)
- Correcting Another Person (or Giving Criticism)

- Getting Another Person's Attention
- Getting the Teacher's Attention
- Giving Compliments
- Greeting Others
- Ignoring Distractions
- Initiating a Conversation
- Interrupting Appropriately
- Introducing Others
- Listening to Others
- Maintaining a Conversation
- Maintaining an Appropriate Appearance
- Making a Phone Call
- Making a Request (Asking a Favor)
- Making Positive Self-Statements
- Making Positive Statements about Others
- Offering Assistance or Help
- Participating in Activities
- Reporting Other Youths' Behavior (or Peer Reporting)
- Resisting Peer Pressure
- Responding to Persons of Authority
- Saying Goodbye to Guest
- Saying "No" Assertively
- Seeking Positive Attention
- Sharing Something
- Showing Appreciation
- Showing Interest
- Sticking Up for Yourself
- Switching from One Task to Another

Autism Spectrum Disorder (Cont.)

- Trying New Tasks
- Using an Appropriate Voice Tone (or Level)
- Using Anger Control Strategies
- Using Structured Problem-Solving (SODAS)
- Using Table Etiquette
- Volunteering
- Waiting Your Turn
- Working with Others

ADVANCED SKILLS
- Accepting Defeat or Loss
- Accepting Help or Assistance
- Accepting Winning Appropriately
- Advocating for Yourself
- Analyzing Skills Needed for Different Situations
- Analyzing Social Situations
- Compromising with Others
- Contributing to Group Activities
- Controlling Emotions
- Cooperating with Others
- Coping with Anger and Aggression from Others
- Coping with Change
- Coping with Conflict
- Coping with Sad Feelings (or Depression)
- Dealing with Accusations
- Dealing with Being Left Out
- Dealing with Boredom
- Dealing with Contradictory Messages
- Dealing with Embarrassing Situations

- Dealing with Failure
- Dealing with Fear
- Dealing with Frustration
- Dealing with Group Pressure
- Dealing with Rejection
- Delaying Gratification
- Displaying Effort
- Displaying Sportsmanship
- Expressing Appropriate Affection
- Expressing Feelings Appropriately
- Expressing Optimism
- Expressing Pride in Accomplishments
- Following Through on Agreements and Contracts
- Gaining Consent
- Giving Consent
- Giving Instructions
- Giving Rationales
- Interacting Appropriately with the Opposite Sex
- Lending to Others
- Making New Friends
- Making Restitution (Compensating)
- Negotiating with Others
- Preparing for a Stressful Conversation
- Preventing Trouble with Others
- Problem-Solving a Disagreement
- Responding to Complaints
- Responding to Others' Feelings
- Responding to Others' Humor
- Responding to Teasing
- Self-Correcting Your Own Behaviors
- Self-Reporting Your Own Behaviors

Autism Spectrum Disorder (Cont.)

- Setting Appropriate Boundaries
- Sharing Attention with Others
- Sharing Personal Experiences
- Suggesting an Activity
- Using Appropriate Humor
- Using Relaxation Strategies
- Using Self-Talk or Self-Instruction
- Using Spontaneous Problem-Solving

COMPLEX SKILLS

- Accepting Yourself
- Altering Your Environment
- Asking for Advice
- Assessing Your Own Abilities
- Being Assertive
- Being Patient
- Differentiating Friends from Acquaintances
- Displaying Appropriate Control
- Expressing Empathy and Understanding for Others
- Expressing Grief
- Identifying Your Own Feelings
- Laughing at Yourself
- Maintaining Relationships
- Making an Appropriate Complaint
- Managing Stress
- Recognizing Moods of Others
- Resolving Conflicts
- Taking Risks Appropriately
- Using Self-Monitoring and Self-Reflection

ATTENTION-DEFICIT/HYPERACTIVITY DISORDERS

Attention-Deficit/Hyperactivity Disorder
Other Specified Attention-Deficit/Hyperactivity Disorder
Unspecified Attention-Deficit/Hyperactivity Disorder

Suggested Social Skills Training for Individuals Diagnosed with an Attention-Deficit/ Hyperactivity Disorder

BASIC SKILLS

- Accepting Criticism (Feedback) or a Consequence
- Accepting "No" for an Answer
- Adjusting Behavior Based on Social Cues
- Being Prepared for Class
- Being Safe Online
- Disagreeing Appropriately
- Following Instructions
- Following through on Agreements and Contracts
- Gaining Consent
- Making Decisions
- Problem-Solving a Disagreement
- Reading Social Cues
- Responding to Written Requests
- Showing Respect
- Using Study Skills
- Using Technology Appropriately

INTERMEDIATE SKILLS

- Accepting Compliments
- Accepting Consequences
- Accepting Decisions of Authority
- Agreeing to Disagree
- Asking for Permission
- Asking for Time to Cool Down
- Being on Time (Promptness)

- Checking In (or Checking Back)
- Choosing Appropriate Words
- Completing Homework
- Completing Tasks
- Complying with a Reasonable Request
- Doing Good Quality Work
- Following Written Instructions
- Getting Another Person's Attention
- Getting the Teacher's Attention
- Ignoring Distractions
- Interrupting Appropriately
- Listening to Others
- Resisting Peer Pressure
- Responding to Persons of Authority
- Saying "No" Assertively
- Seeking Positive Attention
- Sharing Something
- Staying on Task
- Sticking Up for Others
- Sticking Up for Yourself
- Switching from One Task to Another
- Using an Appropriate Voice Tone (or Level)
- Using Anger Control Strategies
- Using Structured Problem-Solving (SODAS)
- Waiting Your Turn
- Working with Others

Attention-Deficit/Hyperactivity Disorders (Cont.)

ADVANCED SKILLS

- Accepting Defeat or Loss
- Accepting Winning Appropriately
- Adjusting Behavior Based on Social Cues
- Analyzing Skills Needed for Different Situations
- Analyzing Social Situations
- Analyzing Tasks to Be Completed
- Being Prepared for Class
- Being Safe Online
- Concentrating on a Subject or Task
- Controlling Emotions
- Coping with Anger and Aggression from Others
- Coping with Conflict
- Dealing with Being Left Out
- Dealing with Boredom
- Dealing with Failure
- Dealing with Frustration
- Dealing with Group Pressure
- Dealing with Rejection
- Delaying Gratification
- Displaying Effort
- Displaying Sportsmanship
- Expressing Feelings Appropriately
- Following Through on Agreements and Contracts
- Gaining Consent
- Making Decisions
- Managing Time
- Organizing Tasks and Activities
- Persevering on Tasks and Projects
- Preventing Trouble with Others

- Problem-Solving a Disagreement
- Reading Social Cues
- Responding to Complaints
- Responding to Teasing
- Responding to Written Requests
- Self-Correcting Your Own Behaviors
- Sharing Attention with Others
- Using Appropriate Humor
- Using Spontaneous Problem-Solving
- Using Study Skills
- Using Technology Appropriately
- Working Independently

COMPLEX SKILLS

- Altering Your Environment
- Being Assertive
- Being Patient
- Budgeting and Managing Money
- Displaying Appropriate Control
- Formulating Strategies
- Gathering Information
- Managing Stress
- Planning Ahead
- Resolving Conflicts
- Setting Goals
- Taking Risks Appropriately
- Using Leisure Time
- Using Self-Monitoring and Self-Reflection

SPECIFIC LEARNING DISORDER

Suggested Social Skills Training for Individuals Diagnosed with a Learning Disorder

BASIC SKILLS

- Accepting Criticism (Feedback) or a Consequence
- Following Instructions

INTERMEDIATE SKILLS

- Asking for Clarification
- Asking for Help
- Asking Questions
- Checking In (or Checking Back)
- Choosing Appropriate Words
- Completing Homework
- Completing Tasks
- Doing Good Quality Work
- Following Written Instructions
- Getting the Teacher's Attention
- Ignoring Distractions
- Listening to Others
- Making Positive Self-Statements
- Managing Time
- Participating in Activities
- Sharing Something
- Staying on Task
- Sticking Up for Yourself
- Switching from One Task to Another
- Working with Others

ADVANCED SKILLS

- Accepting Help or Assistance
- Advocating for Yourself
- Analyzing Skills Needed for Different Situations

- Analyzing Tasks to Be Completed
- Being Prepared for Class
- Concentrating on a Subject or Task
- Contributing to Group Activities
- Controlling Emotions
- Dealing with Failure
- Dealing with Frustration
- Displaying Effort
- Expressing Feelings Appropriately
- Expressing Optimism
- Expressing Pride in Accomplishments
- Making Decisions
- Organizing Tasks and Activities
- Persevering on Tasks and Projects
- Responding to Teasing
- Responding to Written Requests
- Self-Correcting Your Own Behaviors
- Using Relaxation Strategies
- Using Self-Talk or Self-Instruction
- Using Study Skills
- Working Independently

COMPLEX SKILLS

- Accepting Yourself
- Asking for Advice
- Assessing Your Own Abilities
- Being Patient
- Budgeting and Managing Money
- Formulating Strategies
- Gathering Information
- Giving Rationales
- Interviewing for a Job

Specific Learning Disorder (Cont.)

- Managing Stress
- Planning Ahead
- Rewarding Yourself
- Setting Goals
- Using Community Resources
- Using Self-Monitoring and Self-Reflection
- Using Strategies to Find a Job

MOTOR DISORDERS

Developmental Coordination Disorder
Stereotypic Movement Disorder
Tourette's Disorder
Persistent Motor or Vocal Tic Disorder
Provisional Tic Disorder
Other Specified Tic Disorder
Unspecified Tic Disorder

Suggested Social Skills Training for Individuals Diagnosed with a Motor Disorder

BASIC SKILLS

- Talking with Others

INTERMEDIATE SKILLS

- Making Positive Self-Statements
- Sticking Up for Yourself
- Switching from One Task to Another

ADVANCED SKILLS

- Controlling Emotions
- Coping with Conflict
- Dealing with Embarrassing Situations
- Dealing with Frustration
- Dealing with Rejection
- Expressing Feelings Appropriately
- Preparing for a Stressful Conversation
- Responding to Teasing
- Self-Correcting Your Own Behaviors
- Using Relaxation Strategies

COMPLEX SKILLS

- Accepting Yourself
- Altering Your Environment
- Displaying Appropriate Control
- Managing Stress
- Rewarding Yourself
- Seeking Professional Assistance
- Setting Goals
- Using Self-Monitoring and Self-Reflection

STEREOTYPIC MOVEMENT DISORDER

Suggested Social Skills Training for Individuals Diagnosed with Stereotypic Movement Disorder

BASIC SKILLS

- Accepting Criticism (Feedback) or a Consequence
- Accepting "No" for an Answer
- Disagreeing Appropriately

INTERMEDIATE SKILLS

- Accepting Consequences
- Accepting Decisions of Authority
- Asking for Help
- Complying with a Reasonable Request
- Getting Another Person's Attention
- Getting the Teacher's Attention
- Making a Request (Asking a Favor)
- Making Positive Self-Statements
- Saying "No" Assertively
- Seeking Positive Attention
- Sticking up for yourself
- Switching from One Task to Another
- Using Anger Control Strategies
- Using Structured Problem-Solving (SODAS)

ADVANCED SKILLS

- Controlling Emotions
- Coping with Anger and Aggression from Others
- Coping with Change
- Coping with Conflict
- Coping with Sad Feelings (or Depression)
- Dealing with an Accusation

- Dealing with Being Left Out
- Dealing with Boredom
- Dealing with Failure
- Dealing with Fear
- Dealing with Frustration
- Dealing with Rejection
- Expressing Feelings Appropriately
- Preparing for a Stressful Conversation
- Preventing Trouble with Others
- Problem-Solving a Disagreement
- Responding to Complaints
- Responding to Teasing
- Self-Correcting Your Own Behaviors
- Self-Reporting Your Own Behaviors
- Sharing Attention with Others
- Using Relaxation Strategies
- Using Spontaneous Problem-Solving

COMPLEX SKILLS

- Accepting Yourself
- Displaying Appropriate Control
- Formulating Strategies
- Managing Stress
- Rewarding Yourself
- Seeking Professional Assistance
- Setting Goals
- Using Leisure Time
- Using Self-Monitoring and Self-Reflection

SCHIZOPHRENIA SPECTRUM AND OTHER PSYCHOTIC DISORDERS

Schizophrenia
Schizotypal Disorder
Brief Psychotic Disorder
Schizophreniform Disorder
Schizoaffective Disorder
Delusional Disorder
Other Specified Psychotic Disorder
Unspecified Psychotic Disorder
Substance or Medication-Induced Psychotic Disorder
Psychotic Disorder Due to Another Medical Condition

Suggested Social Skills Training for Individuals Diagnosed with Schizophrenia, Schizophreniform Disorder, or Schizoaffective Disorder

BASIC SKILLS

- Accepting Criticism (Feedback) or a Consequence
- Accepting "No" for an Answer
- Disagreeing Appropriately
- Following Instructions
- Introducing Yourself
- Showing Respect
- Showing Sensitivity to Others
- Talking with Others

INTERMEDIATE SKILLS

- Accepting Compliments
- Accepting Consequences
- Agreeing to Disagree
- Asking for Help
- Asking for Permission
- Asking for Time to Cool Down

- Asking Questions
- Checking In (or Checking Back)
- Choosing Appropriate Words
- Closing a Conversation
- Completing Tasks
- Complying with a Reasonable Request
- Contributing to a Discussion (Joining in a Conversation)
- Doing Good Quality Work
- Getting Another Person's Attention
- Greeting Others
- Initiating a Conversation
- Introducing Others
- Listening to Others
- Maintaining a Conversation
- Maintaining an Appropriate Appearance

Schizophrenia Spectrum and Other Psychotic Disorders (Cont.)

- Maintaining Personal Hygiene
- Making Positive Self-Statements
- Making Positive Statements about Others
- Participating in Activities
- Responding to Persons of Authority
- Saying Goodbye to Guest
- Sharing Something
- Showing Appreciation
- Showing Interest
- Trying New Tasks
- Using an Appropriate Voice Tone (or Level)
- Using Structured Problem-Solving (SODAS)
- Working with Others

ADVANCED SKILLS

- Accepting Defeat or Loss
- Accepting Help or Assistance
- Adjusting Behavior based on Social Cues
- Advocating for Yourself
- Analyzing Skills Needed for Different Situations
- Analyzing Social Situations
- Concentrating on a Subject or Task
- Contributing to Group Activities
- Controlling Emotions
- Coping with Change
- Coping with Conflict
- Coping with Sad Feelings (or Depression)

- Dealing with Being Left Out
- Dealing with Boredom
- Dealing with Embarrassing Situations
- Dealing with Failure
- Dealing with Fear
- Dealing with Frustration
- Dealing with Rejection
- Displaying Effort
- Expressing Feelings Appropriately
- Expressing Optimism
- Following Safety Rules
- Gaining Consent
- Giving Consent
- Making Decisions
- Managing Time
- Negotiating with Others
- Organizing Tasks and Activities
- Persevering on Tasks and Projects
- Preparing for a Stressful Conversation
- Reading Social Cues
- Responding to Teasing
- Responding to the Feelings of Others
- Self-Correcting Your Own Behaviors
- Self-Reporting Your Own Behaviors
- Sharing Personal Experiences
- Using Relaxation Strategies
- Using Self-Talk or Self-Instruction
- Using Spontaneous Problem-Solving
- Using Technology Appropriately
- Working Independently

Schizophrenia Spectrum and Other Psychotic Disorders (Cont.)

COMPLEX SKILLS

- Accepting Yourself
- Altering Your Environment
- Asking for Advice
- Assessing Your Own Abilities
- Budgeting and Managing Money
- Clarifying Values and Beliefs
- Displaying Appropriate Control
- Expressing Empathy and Understanding for Others
- Formulating Strategies
- Gathering Information
- Identifying Your Own Feelings
- Interrupting or Changing Negative or Harmful Thoughts
- Interviewing for a Job
- Laughing at Yourself
- Maintaining Relationships
- Making Moral and Spiritual Decisions
- Managing Stress
- Recognizing Your Own Personal Bias or Opinions
- Responding to Law Enforcement/ Police Interactions
- Rewarding Yourself
- Seeking Professional Assistance
- Setting Goals
- Using Community Resources
- Using Leisure Time
- Using Self-Monitoring and Self-Reflection
- Using Strategies to Find a Job

BIPOLAR AND RELATED DISORDERS

Suggested Social Skills Training for Individuals Diagnosed with Bipolar and Related Disorders

BASIC SKILLS

- Accepting Criticism (Feedback) or a Consequence
- Disagreeing Appropriately
- Engaging with Peers Appropriately
- Following Instructions
- Identifying Feelings
- Showing Respect
- Showing Sensitivity to Others
- Understanding Self
- Using Appropriate Language

INTERMEDIATE SKILLS

- Asking for Help
- Following Rules
- Checking In (or Checking Back)
- Completing One Task at a Time
- Complying with a Reasonable Request
- Contributing to a Discussion (Joining in a Conversation)
- Controlling Emotional Outbursts
- Displaying Critical Thinking Before Acting on Thoughts
- Doing Good Quality Work
- Initiating a Conversation
- Listening to Others
- Maintaining a Conversation
- Maintaining an Appropriate Appearance
- Maintaining Personal Hygiene
- Maintaining Proper Voice Tone and Tempo

- Making Positive Self-Statements
- Participating in Activities
- Showing Appreciation
- Using Coping Strategies
- Using Organizational Strategies
- Using Self-Regulation Techniques
- Using Structured Problem-Solving (SODAS)
- Weighing Options

ADVANCED SKILLS

- Accepting Help or Assistance
- Advocating for Yourself
- Analyzing Skills Needed for Different Situations
- Analyzing Social Situations
- Contributing to Group Activities
- Controlling Emotions
- Controlling Impulses and Cravings
- Coping with Change
- Coping with Conflict
- Coping with Sad Feelings (or Depression)
- Dealing with Boredom
- Dealing with Failure
- Dealing with Fear
- Dealing with Frustration
- Dealing with Rejection
- Displaying Effort
- Expressing Feelings Appropriately
- Following Safety Rules

Bipolar and Related Disorders (Cont.)

- Interrupting or Changing Negative or Harmful Thoughts
- Making Decisions
- Making Friends
- Managing Time
- Organizing Tasks and Activities
- Self-Correcting Your Own Behaviors
- Self-Reporting Your Own Behaviors
- Using Relaxation Strategies
- Using Self-Monitoring Techniques
- Using Self-Talk or Self-Instruction
- Using Spontaneous Problem-Solving

COMPLEX SKILLS

- Accepting Yourself
- Altering Your Environment
- Asking for Advice
- Assessing Your Own Abilities
- Budgeting and Managing Money
- Displaying Appropriate Control
- Interrupting or Changing Negative or Harmful Thoughts
- Interviewing for a Job
- Laughing at Yourself
- Maintaining Relationships
- Managing Stress
- Rewarding Yourself
- Seeking Professional Assistance
- Setting Goals
- Using Community Resources
- Using Leisure Time
- Using Self-Reflection
- Using Strategies to Find a Job

MAJOR DEPRESSIVE DISORDER

Suggested Social Skills Training for Individuals Diagnosed with Major Depressive Disorder

BASIC SKILLS

- Building Self-Esteem
- Identifying Areas of Interest/Skills/ Hobbies
- Identifying Feelings
- Identifying Trusted Supports
- Recognizing Cues and Symptoms of Depressive Episodes

INTERMEDIATE SKILLS

- Building Positive Relationships
- Developing a Plan for Dealing with Depressive Episodes
- Developing Vocabulary to Express Feelings
- Engaging in Healthy Alternative Habits
- Engaging in Positive Self-Talk
- Identifying Stressors
- Initiating Support from Trusted Adults
- Practicing Gratitude
- Practicing Self-Acceptance
- Processing Emotions
- Using Coping Strategies
- Using Relaxation Techniques

ADVANCED SKILLS

- Correcting Distorted Thoughts in Social Settings
- Identifying Personal Needs and Goals
- Identifying Personal Strengths and Contributions
- Maintaining Healthy Relationships

- Participating in Positive Social Situations
- Preparing to Handle Anticipated Stressors
- Recognizing the Cycle of Thoughts, Feelings, and Actions
- Using Assertiveness Techniques
- Using Positive Self-Talk and Positive Thinking

COMPLEX SKILLS

- Accepting Support from Others
- Asking for Support when Needed
- Building Positive Sense of Self
- Creating Action Plans to Meet Goals
- Engaging in Self-Advocacy
- Identifying and Adjusting Negative Interpersonal Patterns
- Interrupting or Changing Negative or Harmful Thoughts
- Participating in Healthy Social Engagements
- Recognizing and Adjusting Irrational Thoughts in Social Settings
- Using Conflict Resolution Strategies
- Using Problem-Solving Strategies

Anxiety Disorders

Generalized Anxiety Disorder
Separation Anxiety
Selective Mutism
Specific Phobia
Social Anxiety Disorder
Panic Disorder
Panic Attack
Agoraphobia
Anxiety Due to Another Medical Condition
Other Specified Anxiety Disorder
Unspecified Anxiety Disorder

Suggested Social Skills Training for Individuals Diagnosed with Anxiety Disorders

BASIC SKILLS

- Introducing Yourself
- Talking with Others

INTERMEDIATE SKILLS

- Accepting Compliments
- Accepting Consequences
- Acknowledging Peer-Initiated Interaction
- Answering Questions Appropriately
- Asking for Help
- Asking Relevant Questions
- Commenting Appropriately in Response to Statements
- Contributing to a Discussion (Joining in a Conversation)
- Cooperating without Prompting

- Demonstrating Confidence When Interacting with Peers
- Engaging in Conversational Turn-Taking
- Engaging in Interactive Play
- Getting Another Person's Attention
- Getting the Teacher's Attention
- Greeting Others
- Identifying Strategies to Reduce Anxiety and Worry in Social Settings
- Initiating a Conversation
- Introducing Others
- Inviting Peers to Play
- Maintaining a Conversation
- Participating in Activities
- Saying "No" Assertively

Anxiety Disorders (Cont.)

ADVANCED SKILLS

- Analyzing Skills Needed for Different Situations
- Analyzing Social Situations
- Contributing to Group Activities
- Demonstrating Effective Problem-Solving
- Describing Decision-Making Steps
- Displaying Effort
- Expressing Feelings Appropriately
- Making New Friends
- Preparing for a Stressful Conversation
- Responding Appropriately to Peer Pressure
- Responding to Others' Feelings
- Responding to Teasing
- Using Self-Talk or Self-Instruction

COMPLEX SKILLS

- Being Assertive
- Expressing Yourself Appropriately when Boundaries are Pushed
- Identifying Actions Needed to Improve Interpersonal Skills
- Identifying Passive, Aggressive, and Assertive Behaviors
- Setting Goals
- Taking Risks Appropriately
- Using Coping Skills to Reduce Stress and Worry in Social Situations
- Using Self-Monitoring and Self-Reflection

Separation Anxiety Disorder

Suggested Social Skills Training for Individuals Diagnosed with Separation Anxiety Disorder

BASIC SKILLS

- Talking with Others

INTERMEDIATE SKILLS

- Asking for Help
- Seeking Positive Attention
- Sticking Up for Yourself

ADVANCED SKILLS

- Controlling Emotions
- Coping with Change
- Dealing with Fear
- Expressing Feelings Appropriately
- Expressing Optimism
- Self-Correcting Your Own Behaviors
- Using Relaxation Strategies
- Using Self-Talk or Self-Instruction

COMPLEX SKILLS

- Displaying Appropriate Control
- Formulating Strategies
- Managing Stress
- Planning Ahead
- Rewarding Yourself
- Setting Goals
- Taking Risks Appropriately
- Using Self-Monitoring and Self-Reflection

Selective Mutism

Suggested Social Skills Training for Individuals Diagnosed with Selective Mutism

BASIC SKILLS

- Introducing Yourself
- Talking with Others

INTERMEDIATE SKILLS

- Accepting Compliments
- Accepting Consequences
- Answering the Phone
- Asking for Help
- Asking for Permission
- Asking for Time to Cool Down
- Asking Questions
- Choosing Appropriate Words
- Closing a Conversation
- Contributing to a Discussion (Joining in a Conversation)
- Getting Another Person's Attention
- Getting the Teacher's Attention
- Greeting Others
- Initiating a Conversation
- Introducing Others
- Maintaining a Conversation
- Participating in Activities
- Responding to Persons of Authority
- Saying "No" Assertively
- Sharing Something
- Showing Appreciation
- Showing Interest
- Sticking Up for Yourself
- Working with Others

ADVANCED SKILLS

- Analyzing Skills Needed for Different Situations
- Analyzing Social Situations
- Being Prepared for Class
- Caring for Your Own Belongings
- Contributing to Group Activities
- Displaying Effort
- Expressing Feelings Appropriately
- Gaining Consent
- Giving Consent
- Making New Friends
- Preparing for a Stressful Conversation
- Responding to Others' Feelings
- Responding to Others' Humor
- Responding to Teasing
- Using Self-Talk or Self-Instruction

COMPLEX SKILLS

- Being Assertive
- Formulating Strategies
- Managing Stress
- Planning Ahead
- Rewarding Yourself
- Setting Goals
- Taking Risks Appropriately
- Using Self-Monitoring and Self-Reflection

OBSESSIVE-COMPULSIVE/RELATED DISORDERS

Suggested Social Skills Training for Individuals Diagnosed with Obsessive-Compulsive/ Related Disorders

BASIC SKILLS

- Accepting Decisions of Authority
- Following Instructions
- Identifying Feelings
- Talking with Others

INTERMEDIATE SKILLS

- Asking for Help
- Preparing to Handle Anticipated Stressors
- Recognizing Stressors
- Recognizing the Cycle of Thoughts, Feelings, and Actions
- Recognizing the Need for a Break
- Reducing Risk of Exposure to Stressors
- Trying New Tasks
- Using Coping Strategies
- Using Relaxation Strategies
- Using Structured Problem-Solving (SODAS)

ADVANCED SKILLS

- Accepting Help or Assistance
- Advocating for Yourself
- Coping with Change
- Dealing with Fear
- Dealing with Frustration
- Delaying Gratification
- Managing Impulses
- Preparing for a Stressful Activity
- Self-Correcting Your Own Behaviors

- Self-Reporting Your Own Behaviors
- Setting Appropriate Boundaries with Self
- Using Distractions to Avoid Compulsive Behaviors
- Using Relaxation Strategies
- Using Self-Talk or Self-Instruction
- Using Spontaneous Problem-Solving

COMPLEX SKILLS

- Accepting Yourself
- Accepting Unknowns
- Altering Your Environment
- Asking for Advice
- Assessing Your Own Needs
- Controlling Compulsive Thoughts/ Behaviors
- Displaying Appropriate Control
- Interrupting or Changing Negative or Harmful Thoughts
- Maintaining Relationships
- Managing Stress
- Taking Risks Appropriately
- Using Alternative Thinking Strategies
- Using Self-Monitoring and Self-Reflection
- Using Self-Talk

TRAUMA- AND STRESSOR-RELATED DISORDERS

Reactive Attachment Disorder
Disinhibited Social Engagement Disorder
Post-Traumatic Stress Disorder
Acute Stress Disorder
Adjustment Disorders
Other Specified Trauma- and Stressor-Related Disorder
Unspecified Specified Trauma- and Stressor-Related
  Disorder

Suggested Social Skills Training for Individuals Diagnosed with Trauma- and Stressor-Related Disorders

BASIC SKILLS

- Greeting Others
- Identifying Trusted Supports
- Introducing Yourself

INTERMEDIATE SKILLS

- Being Flexible with Changes in Routines and Plans
- Cooperating with Others
- Developing a Plan for Dealing with Stressors
- Developing Vocabulary to Express Feelings
- Engaging in Conversation
- Identifying Stressors
- Initiating Support from Trusted Adults
- Processing Emotions
- Regulating Emotions
- Using Relaxation Techniques

ADVANCED SKILLS

- Correcting Distorted Thoughts in Social Settings
- Identifying Coping Strategies
- Identifying Personal Needs and Goals
- Preparing to Handle Anticipated Stressors
- Recognizing the Cycle of Thoughts, Feelings, and Actions
- Reducing Risk of Accidental Exposure to Stressors
- Using Assertiveness Techniques
- Using Positive Self-Talk and Positive Thinking

COMPLEX SKILLS

- Building Positive Sense of Self
- Creating Action Plans to Meet Goals
- Engaging in Self-Advocacy
- Interrupting or Changing Negative or Harmful Thoughts
- Recognizing and Adjusting Irrational Thoughts in Social Settings
- Using Problem-Solving Strategies

Reactive Attachment Disorder of Infancy or Early Childhood

Suggested Social Skills Training for Individuals Diagnosed with Reactive Attachment Disorder

BASIC SKILLS

- Accepting Criticism (Feedback) or a Consequence
- Introducing Yourself
- Showing Respect
- Showing Sensitivity to Others
- Talking with Others

INTERMEDIATE SKILLS

- Accepting Apologies from Others
- Accepting Compliments
- Accepting Consequences
- Accepting Decisions of Authority
- Asking for Help
- Asking for Time to Cool Down
- Checking In (or Checking Back)
- Closing a Conversation
- Complying with a Reasonable Request
- Contributing to a Discussion (Joining in a Conversation)
- Correcting Another Person (or Giving Criticism)
- Getting Another Person's Attention
- Getting the Teacher's Attention
- Giving Compliments
- Greeting Others
- Initiating a Conversation
- Interrupting Appropriately
- Introducing Others
- Listening to Others
- Maintaining a Conversation
- Making an Apology

- Making a Request (Asking a Favor)
- Making Positive Self-Statements
- Making Positive Statements about Others
- Offering Assistance or Help
- Participating in Activities
- Responding to Persons of Authority
- Saying Goodbye to Guest
- Saying "No" Assertively
- Seeking Positive Attention
- Sharing Something
- Showing Appreciation
- Showing Interest
- Using Anger Control Strategies
- Using Structured Problem-Solving (SODAS)
- Volunteering
- Waiting Your Turn
- Working with Others

ADVANCED SKILLS

- Accepting Help or Assistance
- Analyzing Skills Needed for Different Situations
- Analyzing Social Situations
- Being Prepared for Class
- Caring for Others' Property
- Caring for Your Own Belongings
- Choosing Appropriate Friends
- Communicating Honestly
- Compromising with Others
- Controlling Emotions

Reactive Attachment Disorder of Infancy or Early Childhood (Cont.)

- Controlling the Impulse to Lie
- Controlling the Impulse to Steal
- Coping with Change
- Coping with Conflict
- Coping with Sad Feelings (or Depression)
- Dealing with an Accusation
- Dealing with Frustration
- Expressing Appropriate Affection
- Expressing Feelings Appropriately
- Expressing Optimism
- Following Through on Agreements and Contracts
- Making New Friends
- Making Restitution (Compensating)
- Negotiating with Others
- Preparing for a Stressful Conversation
- Preventing Trouble with Others
- Problem-Solving a Disagreement
- Responding to Complaints
- Responding to Others' Feelings
- Self-Correcting Your Own Behaviors
- Self-Reporting Your Own Behaviors
- Setting Appropriate Boundaries
- Sharing Personal Experiences
- Using Self-Talk or Self-Instruction

COMPLEX SKILLS

- Accepting Yourself
- Asking for Advice
- Being an Appropriate Role Model
- Being Assertive
- Differentiating Friends from Acquaintances
- Displaying Appropriate Control
- Expressing Empathy and Understanding for Others
- Expressing Grief
- Formulating Strategies
- Managing Stress
- Planning Ahead

POST-TRAUMATIC STRESS DISORDER
Suggested Social Skills Training for Individuals Diagnosed with Post-Traumatic Stress Disorder

BASIC SKILLS
- Greeting Others
- Identifying Trusted Supports
- Interpreting Nonverbal Clues
- Using Appropriate Nonverbal Cues

INTERMEDIATE SKILLS
- Being Flexible with Changes in Routines and Plans
- Cooperating with Others
- Developing a Plan for Dealing with Stressors
- Developing Awareness of Self in Social Settings
- Developing Vocabulary to Express Feelings
- Engaging in Conversation
- Forming Positive Connections
- Identifying Positive Traits in Others
- Identifying Stressors
- Initiating Support from Trusted Adults
- Processing Emotions
- Regulating Emotions
- Showing Empathy
- Strengthening Active Listening
- Using an Appropriate Voice Tone (or Level)
- Using Appropriate Intonation
- Using Relaxation Techniques

ADVANCED SKILLS
- Controlling Impulses
- Correcting Distorted Thoughts in Social Settings
- Establishing and Maintaining Friendships
- Greeting Others
- Identifying Coping Strategies
- Identifying Personal Needs and Goals
- Identifying Trusted Supports
- Increasing Awareness of Defensive Behaviors
- Interpreting Nonverbal Cues
- Preparing to Handle Anticipated Stressors with Individualized Strategies
- Recognizing the Cycle of Thoughts, Feelings, and Actions
- Reducing Risk of Accidental Exposure to Stressors
- Using Appropriate Nonverbal Cues
- Using Assertiveness Techniques
- Using Positive Self-Talk and Positive Thinking

Post-Traumatic Stress Disorder (Cont.)

COMPLEX SKILLS

- Addressing Issues of Trust
- Building Positive Sense of Self
- Creating Action Plans to Meet Goals
- Engaging in Self-Advocacy
- Engaging in Social Activities Regularly
- Interrupting or Changing Negative or Harmful Thoughts
- Recognizing and Adjusting Irrational Thoughts in Social Settings
- Using Problem-Solving Strategies

DISRUPTIVE, IMPULSE-CONTROL, AND CONDUCT DISORDERS

Oppositional Defiant Disorder
Intermittent Explosive Disorder
Antisocial Personality Disorder
Pyromania
Kleptomania
Other Specified Disruptive Impulse-Control or
　　Conduct Disorder
Unspecified Disruptive Impulse-Control or
　　Conduct Disorder

Suggested Social Skills Training for Individuals Diagnosed with Disruptive, Impulse-Control, and Conduct Disorder

BASIC SKILLS

- Accepting Criticism (Feedback) or a Consequence
- Accepting "No" for an Answer
- Disagreeing Appropriately
- Following Instructions
- Showing Respect
- Showing Sensitivity to Others
- Talking with Others

INTERMEDIATE SKILLS

- Accepting Consequences
- Accepting Decisions of Authority
- Agreeing to Disagree
- Asking for Permission
- Asking for Time to Cool Down
- Checking In (or Checking Back)
- Choosing Appropriate Words
- Complying with a Reasonable Request

- Following Rules
- Getting Another Person's Attention
- Giving Compliments
- Greeting Others
- Interrupting Appropriately
- Listening to Others
- Making an Apology
- Making Positive Statements about Others
- Offering Assistance or Help
- Refraining from Possessing Contraband or Drugs
- Reporting Other Youths' Behavior (or Peer Reporting)
- Resisting Peer Pressure
- Responding to Persons of Authority
- Saying "No" Assertively
- Sharing Something
- Showing Appreciation
- Showing Interest

Disruptive, Impulse-Control, and Conduct Disorders (Cont.)

- Sticking Up for Others
- Sticking Up for Yourself
- Switching from One Task to Another
- Using an Appropriate Voice Tone (or Level)
- Using Anger Control Strategies
- Using Structured Problem-Solving (SODAS)
- Volunteering
- Working with Others

ADVANCED SKILLS
- Accepting Defeat or Loss
- Accepting Winning Appropriately
- Adjusting Behavior Based on Social Cues
- Analyzing Social Situations
- Borrowing from Others
- Caring for Others' Property
- Caring for Your Own Belongings
- Choosing Appropriate Friends
- Communicating Honestly
- Complying with School Dress Code
- Compromising with Others
- Controlling Emotions
- Controlling Sexually Abusive Impulses toward Others
- Controlling the Impulse to Lie
- Controlling the Impulse to Steal
- Cooperating with Others
- Coping with Anger and Aggression from Others
- Coping with Conflict

- Dealing with an Accusation
- Dealing with Boredom
- Dealing with Frustration
- Dealing with Group Pressure
- Dealing with Rejection
- Delaying Gratification
- Displaying Effort
- Expressing Appropriate Affection
- Expressing Feelings Appropriately
- Following Safety Rules
- Following Through on Agreements and Contracts
- Gaining Consent
- Interacting Appropriately with the Opposite Sex
- Keeping Property in Its Place
- Making Decisions
- Making New Friends
- Making Restitution (Compensating)
- Negotiating with Others
- Preventing Trouble with Others
- Problem-Solving a Disagreement
- Responding to Complaints
- Responding to Others' Feelings
- Responding to Others' Humor
- Responding to Teasing
- Self-Correcting Your Own Behaviors
- Self-Reporting Your Own Behaviors
- Setting Appropriate Boundaries
- Sharing Attention with Others
- Sharing Personal Experiences
- Sticking Up for Yourself

Disruptive, Impulse-Control, and Conduct Disorders (Cont.)

- Using Appropriate Humor
- Using Appropriate Language
- Using Self-Talk or Self-Instruction
- Using Spontaneous Problem-Solving
- Using Study Skills
- Using Technology Appropriately

COMPLEX SKILLS

- Being an Appropriate Role Model
- Being Assertive
- Being Patient
- Clarifying Values and Beliefs
- Differentiating Friends from Acquaintances
- Displaying Appropriate Control
- Expressing Empathy and Understanding for Others
- Formulating Strategies
- Identifying Your Own Feelings
- Interrupting or Changing Negative or Harmful Thoughts
- Maintaining Relationships
- Making Moral and Spiritual Decisions
- Managing Stress
- Planning Ahead
- Recognizing Your Own Personal Bias or Opinions
- Resolving Conflicts
- Responding to Law Enforcement/ Police Interactions
- Seeking Professional Assistance
- Using Leisure Time
- Using Self-Monitoring and Self-Reflection
- Valuing Differences

FEEDING RELATED DISORDERS

Suggested Social Skills Training for Individuals Diagnosed with Disruptive, Impulse-Control, and Conduct Disorder

BASIC SKILLS

- Accepting Criticism (Feedback) or a Consequence
- Developing a Growth Mindset
- Developing a Positive Self Concept
- Identifying Emotions
- Recognizing Strengths
- Talking with Others

INTERMEDIATE SKILLS

- Accepting Failure
- Accepting Support from Others
- Building Self-Esteem
- Engaging with Peers
- Expressing Feelings Appropriately
- Identifying Triggers
- Making Positive Statements about Self
- Resisting Impulses
- Resisting Peer Pressure
- Saying "No" Assertively
- Showing Appreciation
- Using Coping Strategies
- Using Emotional Control Strategies
- Using Structured Problem-Solving (SODAS)

ADVANCED SKILLS

- Communicating Honestly
- Controlling Emotions
- Controlling Impulses
- Coping with Conflict
- Dealing with Group Pressure

- Demonstrating Gratitude
- Following Through on Agreements and Contracts
- Making Friends
- Setting Appropriate Boundaries
- Using Self-Talk

COMPLEX SKILLS

- Accepting Yourself
- Being Assertive
- Interrupting or Changing Negative or Harmful Thoughts
- Seeking Professional Assistance
- Using Self-Monitoring and Self-Reflection

ELIMINATION DISORDERS

Encopresis
Enuresis Other Specified Elimination Disorder
Unspecified Elimination Disorder

Suggested Social Skills Training for Individuals Diagnosed with an Elimination Disorder

BASIC SKILLS

- Accepting Criticism (Feedback) or a Consequence

INTERMEDIATE SKILLS

- Maintaining Personal Hygiene
- Making Positive Self-Statements
- Sticking Up for Yourself

ADVANCED SKILLS

- Advocating for Yourself
- Controlling the Impulse to Lie
- Dealing with an Accusation
- Dealing with Embarrassing Situations
- Dealing with Rejection
- Displaying Effort
- Expressing Feelings Appropriately
- Expressing Optimism
- Making Restitution (Compensating)
- Responding to Teasing
- Self-Reporting Your Own Behaviors
- Sharing Personal Experiences

COMPLEX SKILLS

- Clarifying Values and Beliefs
- Formulating Strategies
- Interrupting or Changing Negative or Harmful Thoughts
- Making Moral and Spiritual Decisions
- Managing Stress
- Planning Ahead
- Rewarding Yourself
- Setting Goals

GENDER DYSPHORIA DISORDERS

Suggested Social Skills Training for Individuals Diagnosed with Gender Dysphoria

BASIC SKILLS

- Identifying Feelings
- Identifying Trusted Supports
- Talking with Others
- Understanding Feelings

INTERMEDIATE SKILLS

- Advocating for Yourself
- Analyzing Social Situations
- Coping with Conflict
- Making Positive Self-Statements
- Using Structured Problem-Solving (SODAS)

ADVANCED SKILLS

- Controlling Emotions
- Coping with Conflict
- Dealing with Fear
- Dealing with Frustration
- Dealing with Rejection
- Expressing Feelings Appropriately
- Making Friends
- Responding to Teasing
- Using Coping Techniques
- Using Relaxation Strategies

COMPLEX SKILLS

- Accepting Yourself
- Displaying Appropriate Control
- Managing Stress
- Rewarding Yourself
- Seeking Professional Assistance
- Using Community Resources
- Using Self-Monitoring and Self-Reflection

Substance-Related Disorders

ALCOHOL-RELATED DISORDERS

Alcohol Dependence
Alcohol Abuse

AMPHETAMINE-RELATED DISORDERS

Amphetamine Dependence
Amphetamine Abuse

CAFFEINE-RELATED DISORDERS

Caffeine Dependence
Caffeine Abuse

CANNABIS-RELATED DISORDERS

Cannabis Dependence
Cannabis Abuse

COCAINE-RELATED DISORDERS

Cocaine Dependence
Cocaine Abuse

HALLUCINOGEN-RELATED DISORDERS

Hallucinogen Dependence
Hallucinogen Abuse

INHALANT-RELATED DISORDERS

Inhalant Dependence
Inhalant Abuse

NICOTINE-RELATED DISORDERS

Nicotine Dependence
Nicotine Abuse

OPIOID-RELATED DISORDERS

Opioid Dependence
Opioid Abuse

PHENCYCLIDINE-RELATED DISORDERS

Phencyclidine Dependence
Phencyclidine Abuse

SEDATIVE-, HYPNOTIC-, OR ANXIOLYTIC-RELATED DISORDERS

Sedative, Hypnotic, or Anxiolytic Dependence
Sedative, Hypnotic, or Anxiolytic Abuse

POLYSUBSTANCE-RELATED DISORDERS

Polysubstance Dependence
Polysubstance Abuse

OTHER (OR UNKNOWN) SUBSTANCE-RELATED DISORDERS

Other (Or Unknown) Substance Dependence
Other (Or Unknown) Substance Abuse

**Suggested Social Skills Training for Individuals Diagnosed with
a Substance-Related Disorder**

BASIC SKILLS

- Talking with Others

INTERMEDIATE SKILLS

- Asking for Help
- Checking In (or Checking Back)
- Following Rules
- Making Positive Self-Statements
- Participating in Activities
- Refraining from Possessing
  Contraband or Drugs
- Reporting Emergencies
- Reporting Other Youths' Behavior
  (or Peer Reporting)
- Resisting Peer Pressure
- Responding to Persons of Authority
- Saying "No" Assertively
- Seeking Positive Attention
- Using Structured Problem-Solving
  (SODAS)
- Working with Others

ADVANCED SKILLS

- Accepting Help or Assistance
- Choosing Appropriate Friends
- Communicating Honestly
- Controlling Emotions
- Coping with Anger and Aggression
  from Others
- Coping with Change
- Coping with Conflict
- Coping with Sad Feelings
  (or Depression)
- Dealing with an Accusation

- Dealing with Boredom
- Dealing with Failure
- Dealing with Frustration
- Dealing with Group Pressure
- Delaying Gratification
- Expressing Feelings Appropriately
- Expressing Optimism
- Expressing Pride in Accomplishments
- Following Safety Rules
- Making Decisions
- Making Restitution (Compensating)
- Preparing for a Stressful Conversation
- Preventing Trouble with Others
- Problem-Solving a Disagreement
- Self-Correcting Your Own Behaviors
- Self-Reporting Your Own Behaviors
- Using Relaxation Strategies
- Using Spontaneous Problem-Solving

COMPLEX SKILLS

- Accepting Yourself
- Altering Your Environment
- Asking for Advice
- Being an Appropriate Role Model
- Being Assertive
- Being Patient
- Clarifying Values and Beliefs
- Differentiating Friends from
  Acquaintances
- Displaying Appropriate Control
- Formulating Strategies
- Identifying Your Own Feelings

Substance-Related Disorders (Cont.)

- Interrupting or Changing Negative or Harmful Thoughts
- Laughing at Yourself
- Maintaining Relationships
- Making Moral and Spiritual Decisions
- Managing Stress
- Planning Ahead
- Responding to Law Enforcement/ Police Interactions
- Rewarding Yourself
- Seeking Professional Assistance
- Setting Goals
- Using Community Resources
- Using Leisure Time
- Using Self-Monitoring and Self-Reflection

Personality Disorders

Cluster A Personality Disorders
Cluster B Personality Disorders
Cluster C Personality Disorders

Suggested Social Skills Training for Individuals Diagnosed with a Personality Disorder

BASIC SKILLS

- Identifying Core Values
- Identifying Feelings
- Talking with Others

INTERMEDIATE SKILLS

- Building a Strong Sense of Self
- Building Healthy Relationships
- Closing a Conversation
- Cooperating with Peers
- Identifying Trusted Peers and Adults
- Initiating a Conversation
- Practicing Mindfulness and Being in the Present Moment
- Regulating Emotions
- Responding with Curiosity
- Saying "No" Assertively
- Setting Appropriate Boundaries
- Using Coping Strategies
- Using Self-Soothing Techniques

ADVANCED SKILLS

- Accepting Help from Supports
- Adjusting Behavior Based on Social Cues
- Analyzing Skills Needed for Different Situations
- Analyzing Social Situations
- Expressing Feelings Appropriately
- Forgiving When Forgiveness is Warranted
- Identifying Distorted Thoughts in Relationships
- Making and Keeping Friends
- Practicing Self-Validation and Self-Acceptance
- Reaching Out to Supports
- Recognizing Unhealthy Relationship Patterns
- Using Distress Tolerance Skills
- Using Self-Talk or Self-Instruction
- Validating Others

Personality Disorders (Cont.)

COMPLEX SKILLS

- Being Assertive
- Interrupting or Changing Negative or Harmful Thoughts
- Maintaining Healthy Boundaries
- Maintaining Strong Healthy Relationships
- Moving Away from Unhealthy Relationships
- Using Alternative and Realistic Thinking Strategies
- Using Problem-Solving Strategies
- Using Self-Monitoring and Self-Reflection

>>> QUICK RECAP

Use of Charts in Treatment Planning Development and Review:

➤ The social skills outlined in the charts are a helpful quick reference when determining social skills in treatment planning.

➤ Use of these charts allows for ease in identification of individual needs and objectives that fit into the cognitively and developmentally appropriate frame.

Useful Tips in Treatment Planning:

➤ Skill selection should be based on specific referral concerns, present levels of performance, and other relevant components rather than solely on the diagnosis.

➤ Individualized needs should drive the determination of treatment plan decisions.

➤ A good treatment plan is the first step to effective treatment.

Chapter 6

Treatment Planning with a Focus on Social Skill Instruction

Treatment planning should be an integral component of the care system in any setting where youth, particularly at-risk youth or those who could benefit from more individually focused supports, receive treatment. All members of a treatment team should work together in order to design the most effective treatment plans to meet the individual needs of each youth. When treatment plans are individualized, well-thought out, and comprehensive, youth are more likely to experience success during treatment, overcome their problems, and lead more successful, fulfilling lives.

This chapter includes an introduction to the treatment planning process and the elements necessary for creative, effective, and therapeutic treatment plans. Four realistic treatment plan examples illustrate how the information in the charts presented in Chapter 5 can be applied in the treatment of children diagnosed with a specific mental health disorder. These plans are typical of those used in a family preservation setting, a school setting, a residential family home setting, and a psychiatric setting, and demonstrate treatment planning across various programs. The social skills prescribed as part of each treatment plan are italicized.

Treatment Planning Process

Treatment planning is a key component in addressing and successfully treating the symptoms and behaviors associated with mental health disorders. The treatment planning process guides treatment providers as they consider an individual's history, their current problems, and how best to deal with and treat those problems. Treatment planning requires a team of treatment providers from various areas of a youth's life to work together and lend their expertise to the process. With a wide range of treatment team members involved, the quality of service provided can be enhanced through unique ideas, perceptions, experiences, and specializations.

Treatment plans are created during a team meeting. In a school setting, a team meeting might include the youth, their parents or caregivers, the youth's teachers, a special education representative, and any other specialized staff involved in the youth's education (speech pathologist, occupational therapist, school psychologist, behavior interventionist, etc.). When home-based services are being provided, a team meeting might simply include the family consultant and the family. In a residential care setting, a team meeting might include the youth, their parents or caregivers, youth care supervisors, youth care workers, and other individuals involved in the youth's treatment (psychiatrist, psychologist, therapist, caseworker, guardian ad litem, probation officer, etc.).

During a meeting, team members discuss and identify the youth's past and current behaviors and symptoms to target for treatment. Based on present issues and problems, the team determines the most appropriate goals for individual youth. The result of the team meeting is a document called a treatment plan.

Several necessary components are included in all treatment plans. First, it's important to include a youth's demographic and historical information. This can include age, gender, race, referral concerns, contact information, insurance numbers, medical history, psychiatric history, developmental history, social history, family history, chemical dependency issues, risk factors (suicidality, homicidality, abuse, etc.), educational history, occupational history (if applicable), and other relevant information. Second, the individual's mental health disorder diagnosis should be stated. Third, the youth's treatment goals (and how social skill instruction can help achieve them) should be specifically stated. Fourth, the objectives for meeting the treatment goals should be clearly defined so that anyone reading the objectives can understand how they relate to the goals, how to measure them, and what progress is anticipated. Fifth, a youth's progress toward their treatment goals since the previous treatment plan should be specifically stated. (This component would not be included if this is the youth's first treatment plan.) Finally, future dates to review progress should be determined and listed in the treatment plan.

Once an individualized treatment plan is complete, it serves as a guide for everyone who works with the youth. It helps ensure that all members of the treatment team are working toward the same goals, provides a method of accountability for the team, and offers a standard against which process can be measured. A treatment plan should be thought of as a "living" document because it can be modified and further developed at each team meeting, depending on a youth's progress. New objectives and goals can be added when needed, while individualized goals that have been achieved can be removed. An individualized treatment plan is the best way to guarantee that services from treatment providers are consistent, effective, and, ultimately, successful.

Using Treatment Plans

Good treatment plans are organized, goal-directed, functional, and fluid. They allow treatment to be provided in a systematic, planned, and focused way, while also providing for flexibility based on the changing climate in a youth's environment. Once a treatment plan is developed, it is important for all to understand, follow, and use the plan throughout the course of a youth's treatment.

Developing a quality treatment plan isn't easy; it requires time and effort to do it right. Sometimes, treatment providers can get bogged down in the required paperwork and the treatment planning process becomes an exercise in simply filling out forms. When the process isn't taken seriously, neither is the resulting treatment plan. That's why it's important for treatment providers to be diligent as they build an effective, comprehensive plan and follow through to ensure that it benefits the youth.

Remember that a treatment plan is a "living" document. This means it can change as the situation warrants. If, after a reasonable amount of time and evaluation, parts of a treatment plan aren't working, it should be adjusted and changed so that it can better meet the youth's needs.

The treatment planning process helps to ensure that youth are receiving treatment that is focused on their specific problems and associated skill deficits. In addition, individual considerations (developmental level, social influence, cultural norms, etc.) should be reflected throughout the treatment plan. By using individualized treatment plans like those presented here, caregivers can provide quality, effective treatment and increase the likelihood that youth will get better.

Example Treatment Plans

In the following pages are the treatment tales of Ethan, Leland, and Iyla. Each of these youth are in need of individualized support, and each is in need for varying reasons. For each case, you will first see a brief synopsis explaining the youth's diagnosis and evidence that led to this conclusion. Next, you will see various artifacts related to the youth's disorders, beginning with an artifact explaining the context that led to an evaluation of the youth and ending with the finalized treatment plan.

ETHAN: Enthusiastic, Energetic, and Vivacious Adventurer with Social, Emotional, Academic, and Behavioral Superhero Potential

Synopsis: Ethan is an eleven-year-old boy who a licensed mental health professional has evaluated and diagnosed as having Attention Deficit/Hyperactivity Disorder (ADHD). Symptoms, present since age 5, are causing Ethan significant problems in school and at home. The diagnosis was based on multiple sources of information, including clinically elevated DISC scores for ADHD; clinically significant scores on the BASC Parent Rating Scale, BASC Teacher Rating Scale, and BASC Self Report of Personality on the Inattention/Hyperactivity Scale; a school observation where Ethan was found to be off task eighty percent of the time; and biological parent and teacher reports of the following DSM-5 diagnostic criteria:

- Has difficulty paying attention or sustaining attention.

- Fails to follow through with instructions.

- Is unable to concentrate on details, resulting in careless mistakes.

- Doesn't listen when spoken to directly.

- Is easily distracted.

- Regularly loses homework and textbooks.

- Drags out or avoids completion of homework or chores at home.

- Constantly interrupts others and blurts out answers before questions have been completed.

- Doesn't wait his turn.

- Often fidgets with hands and feet, and squirms in his chair.

- Often is "on the go" or acts as if "driven by a motor."

- Often has difficulty playing or engaging in leisure activities quietly.

Artifact Samples Below:

- Letter from parents sent post-IEP eligibility meeting in preparation for the initial IEP planning meeting

- Copy of the *Family Preservation Remedial Services Individualized Treatment Plan*

- Copy of the school treatment team-created IEP

>>> LETTER FROM PARENTS

Dear IEP Team,

Thank you for taking the time earlier this month to come together for our son's (Ethan Smith, DOB: 5-17-XXXX) IEP eligibility meeting. We were unsure what to expect following the private evaluation results indicating a diagnosis of ADHD, but we feel very confident in your ability to support Ethan in overcoming the challenges he faces with this diagnosis. We are looking forward to our upcoming planning meeting to determine goals and next steps. As you know, his symptoms are significantly impacting progress and his ability to access the curriculum. We are comforted in knowing that an individualized plan will allow him to grow in all areas.

Although you have copies of the evaluation, notes from Family Consultant Kelly O'Connell, and the paperwork that we completed in preparation for the initial eligibility meeting, we also wanted to share some of our parental concerns, as this may help drive portions of our conversation regarding goals and supporting steps that can be taken both at school and at home. Our main concerns include:

- Ethan's inability to sustain attention or to stay on topic

- lack of attention to details, resulting in careless errors

- impulsive actions such as calling out, interrupting, and distracting peers

- organizational issues such as frequently losing materials and homework

- forgetfulness and other executive functioning deficiencies

- inability to focus on undesirable activities (homework, dinner time, chores, etc.)

- mastery of concepts and classroom objectives are not being demonstrated because he is unable to focus long enough to show his understanding

- emotional outbursts stemming from an inability to articulate his emotions or to understand why he cannot, in his words, "act like my friends and other people in class"

Please let us know if there is any other information that we can prepare before our meeting. We look forward to collaborating with the goal of nurturing our son and giving him what he needs to succeed!

Thank you for your continued support,

Helen and Thomas Smith, Ethan's parents

Family Preservation Remedial Services
Individualized Treatment Plan

CLIENT NAME: Ethan Smith	**PARENT/LEGAL GUARDIAN NAME & ADDRESS:** Helen & Thomas Smith 1234 5th Ave. Village, ST 12345 **PHONE:** 555-123-4567
DOB: 5-17-XXXX **GENDER:** Male	**RELATIONSHIP TO CHILD:** Biological parents
ADDRESS: 1234 5th Ave. Village, ST 12345 **PHONE:** 555-123-4567	**LPHA NAME AND ADDRESS:** Lisa Todd, M.S., LISW Psychological Health 1234 Happy Dr. Village, ST 12345 **PHONE:** 555-765-4321
COUNTY: Fort	**MEDICAID NUMBER:** 12345678
PROVIDER AGENCY: AAA Agency 1234 W. Townsend, SUITE 1 Village, ST 12345 **PHONE:** 555-789-4567 **FAX #:** 555-789-4568	**REMEDIAL SERVICE PROVIDER:** Kelly O'Connell, M.S.
PROVIDER NUMBER: #1234567	**DATE SUBMITTED:** 8-27-20XX

DIAGNOSIS   314.01 Attention-Deficit/Hyperactivity Disorder, combined type
Moderate environmental stressors, including recent move, father currently out of work, and poor academic performance

MEDICATIONS, IF ANY: 15mg of Adderall XR daily

Collaborative Treatment Planning

Collaboration occurred with mental health provider via letter received on 8-23-20XX.

Lisa Todd conducted the mental health assessment on 5-24-20XX and updated the order to include individual units on 8-23-20XX. AAA Agency received the order on 8-23-20XX at 1:38 p.m. The report identified the current target symptoms for Ethan as difficulty remaining on task, difficulty completing homework and tasks, difficulty following instructions, and frequently blurting out and making noises. The mental health provider requested that the focus for Ethan's remedial services include: increasing time on task.

Collaboration occurred with Helen and Thomas Smith on 8-17-20XX.

Helen and Thomas expressed their desire to continue with services as they feel it has helped Ethan improve his behaviors and also has helped hold him accountable. Thomas reports that the services have helped to improve his relationship with his son. Helen identified Ethan's positive attitude as a strength, and Thomas identified Ethan's interest in sports as a strength. Ethan's parents' primary concern is his difficulty with following instructions. Helen and Thomas feel that Ethan needs continued work on improving his ability to follow instructions promptly after they are given and remaining on task until the task is completed.

Collaboration occurred with Ethan Smith on 8-17-20XX.

Ethan is an 11-year-old healthy, Caucasian male. Ethan states that he feels his ability to maintain attention has improved since he recently began taking his new medication. However, he thinks he still needs some work on getting tasks done in a prompt and efficient manner, particularly homework. He reports that he is pleased that he is getting along better with his father, and is enjoying spending time with his father once again. He stated, "Dad is on my case less often when I just get things done." Ethan also feels that he needs to continue working on using self-monitoring skills. Ethan feels that when he does not monitor his behavior, he tends to blurt out more often and do things "without thinking."

Baseline:

Ethan follows 40% of instructions given on an average day.
Ethan completes homework an average of 1 out of 5 school days.
Ethan completes 60% of tasks.
Ethan is on task 20% of the time on an average day.
Ethan blurts out and makes unsolicited noises about 20 times a day.

Discharge Plan:

Ethan will increase instructions followed to at least 70% on average.
Ethan will complete homework 5 out of 5 school days.
Ethan will complete 90% of tasks.
Ethan will increase his on-task time to at least 70% on average.
Ethan will blurt out and make unsolicited noises no more than 5 times a day.

Goals and Objectives of Treatment

Mental Health Diagnosis: Attention-Deficit/Hyperactivity Disorder, combined type
Mental Health Symptoms Identified by the LPHA Requiring Remedial Services: Frequently off task, difficulty completing homework and tasks, difficulty following instructions, and often blurting out and making noises.
Desired Outcome: Ethan will be able to use positive social skills to improve his ability to remain on task, complete homework and tasks, follow instructions, and monitor his impulsive behaviors.

GOAL #1: Ethan will learn social skills to improve his ability to follow instructions.

Objective #1: Ethan will improve his ability to follow instructions by showing more often that he can follow an instruction after the first time it is given without arguing. This will be measured by behavior chart, self-report, parental report, and Family Consultant observation by 11-30-20XX.

Service Activity A (Domains I, F, S): The Family Consultant, Kelly O'Connell, will teach Ethan the social skill of *Following Instructions* when instructions are given verbally and generalize the use of this skill to family and school environments.

Service Activity B (Domains I, S): The Family Consultant, Kelly O'Connell, will teach Ethan the social skill of *Following Written Instructions* and generalize the use of this skill to the school environment.

Service Activity C (Domains I, F, S): The Family Consultant, Kelly O'Connell, will role-play with Ethan the skill of *Following Instructions* and generalize the use of this skill to the family and school environment.

Service Activity D (Domains I): Ethan will report to the Family Consultant how often he is able to successfully use the skills of *Following Instructions* (verbally) and *Following Written Instructions* on a weekly basis.

Service Activity E (Domains I, F): The Family Consultant will teach Ethan's parents how to praise and reinforce Ethan when he follows verbal and written instructions. Ethan will earn points and/or praise for instructions followed and will be allowed to cash in points for rewards daily.

Service Activity F (Domains F): Helen and Thomas will track Ethan's following-instruction behavior on the daily behavior chart and report to the Family Consultant. **(Non-remedial)**

Service Activity G (Domains F, S): The Family Consultant will teach Helen and Thomas how to obtain daily information from the school regarding Ethan's following-instructions performance. **(Non-remedial)**

GOAL #2: Ethan will learn positive social skills to increase his time on task and completion of tasks.

Objective #1: Ethan will improve his ability to remain on task by showing his intent to be on task without interruption. This will be measured by behavior chart, self-report, parental report, and Family Consultant observation by 11-30-20XX.

Service Activity A (Domains I, F, S, C): The Family Consultant, Kelly O'Connell, will teach Ethan the social skill of *Staying on Task* and generalize the use of this skill to the family, school, and community environments.

Service Activity B (Domains I, F, P, S, C): The Family Consultant, Kelly O'Connell, will teach Ethan the social skill of *Ignoring Distractions* and generalize the use of this skill across all environments.

Service Activity C (Domains I, F, S, C): The Family Consultant, Kelly O'Connell, will teach Ethan the social skill of *Persevering on Tasks and Projects* and generalize the use of this skill to the family, school, and community environments.

Service Activity D (Domains I): Ethan will report to the Family Consultant how often he is able to successfully use the skills of *Staying on Task, Ignoring Distractions,* and *Persevering on Tasks and Projects* on a weekly basis.

Service Activity E (Domains I, F): The Family Consultant will teach Ethan's parents how to praise and reinforce Ethan when he remains on task, ignores distractions by others, and perseveres on tasks and projects. Ethan will earn points and/or praise for social skills exhibited and will be allowed to cash in points for rewards daily.

Service Activity F (Domains F): Helen and Thomas will track Ethan's on-task behavior on the daily behavior chart and report to the Family Consultant. **(Non-remedial)**

Service Activity G (Domains F, S): The Family Consultant will teach Helen and Thomas how to obtain daily information from the school regarding Ethan's on-task behavior. **(Non-remedial)**

Objective #2: Ethan will improve his ability to complete tasks by showing an increase in completed assignments and chores. This will be measured by behavior chart, self-report, parental report, and Family Consultant observation by 11-30-20XX.

Service Activity A (Domains I, F, S): The Family Consultant, Kelly O'Connell, will teach Ethan the social skill of *Completing Homework* and generalize the use of this skill to the family and school environments.

Service Activity B (Domains I, F, S): The Family Consultant, Kelly O'Connell, will teach Ethan the social skill of *Completing Tasks* and generalize the use of this skill to the family and school environments.

Service Activity C (Domains I): Ethan will report to the Family Consultant how often he is able to successfully use the skills of *Completing Homework* and *Completing Tasks* on a weekly basis.

Service Activity D (Domains I, F): The Family Consultant will teach Ethan's parents how to praise and reinforce Ethan when he completes homework and tasks. Ethan will earn points and/or praise for social skills exhibited and will be allowed to cash in points for rewards daily.

Service Activity E (Domains F): Helen and Thomas will track Ethan's homework and task-completion behavior on the daily behavior chart and report to the Family Consultant. **(Non-remedial)**

Service Activity F (Domains F, S): The Family Consultant will teach Helen and Thomas how to obtain daily information from the school regarding Ethan's task-completion behavior. **(Non-remedial)**

GOAL #3: Ethan will improve his self-monitoring of impulsive behavior.

Objective #1: Ethan will learn positive social skills to help him improve control of his impulsive behaviors of blurting out and making noises. This will be measured by self-report, parental report, and Family Consultant observation by 11-30-20XX.

Service Activity A (Domains I, F, P, S, C): The Family Consultant, Kelly O'Connell, will teach Ethan the social skill of *Displaying Appropriate Control* and generalize the use of this skill across all environments.

Service Activity B (Domains I, F, P, S, C): The Family Consultant, Kelly O'Connell, will teach Ethan the social skill of *Using Self-Monitoring* and *Self-Reflection* and generalize the use of this skill across all environments.

Service Activity C (Domains I): Ethan will report to the Family Consultant how often he is able to successfully use the skills of *Displaying Appropriate Control* and *Using Self-Monitoring and Self-Reflection* on a weekly basis.

Service Activity D (Domains I, F): The Family Consultant will teach Ethan's parents how to praise and reinforce Ethan when he displays appropriate control and utilizes self-monitoring. Ethan will earn points and/or praise for social skills exhibited and will be allowed to cash in points for rewards daily.

Service Activity E (Domains F): Helen and Thomas will track Ethan's impulsive behavior on the daily behavior chart and report to the Family Consultant. **(Non-remedial)**

Service Activity F (Domains F, S): The Family Consultant will teach Helen and Thomas how to obtain daily information from the school regarding Ethan's impulsive behavior. **(Non-remedial)**

I-Individual, F-Family, P-Peer, S-School, C-Community

This concludes the Implementation Plan.

Individualized Education Plan

NAME: Ethan Smith   **ADDRESS:** 1234 5th Ave., Village, ST 12345

BIRTH DATE: 05/17/XXXX   **CURRENT GRADE:** 6th   **LAST MDT:** February 23, 20XX

DISABILITY
Other Health Impairment
(OHI; diagnosed with
ADHD, combined type)

SCHOOL
Village South
Elementary School

STATE WARD
☐Yes ☒No

PARENT/GUARDIAN
Helen & Thomas Smith

ADDRESS
1234 5th Ave., Village, ST 12345

PHONE
(555) 123-4567

The Parental Rights of Special Education have been reviewed with me, and I have received a copy.

_____   _____

parent/guardian initials   date

**The school district has taken necessary actions to ensure
that I understand the proceedings of this IEP conference.**   ☐ Yes ☐ No

---

RESIDENT DISTRICT
Village Public School District

ADDRESS
1234 Lincoln Street
Village, ST 12345

PHONE
(555) 234-5678

CONTACT PERSON   Kathy Wong, Ph.D.   (555) 345-6789

The following participants attended the IEP conference:

NAME	RELATIONSHIP TO STUDENT
Helen Smith	*Mother*
Kathy Wong	*School Psychologist*
Carl Fine	*Principal*
Rhonda Rogers	*Regular Ed. Reading Teacher*
Paula Cleary	*Regular Ed. Mathematics Teacher*
Mary Prince	*Regular Ed. Social Studies Teacher*
Latoya Johnson	*Regular Ed. Science Teacher*
Sean Harmon	*Guidance Counselor*
Vince Peters	*Regular Ed. Physical Education Teacher*
Simone Benson	*Regular Ed. Language Arts Teacher*
Olivia Sanchez	*Special Ed. Reading & Lang. Arts Teacher*
Mark Franklin	*Special Ed. Math & Science Teacher*
Collin McKinney	*Special Ed. Social Studies & P.E. Teacher*
Christina Temple	*Special Ed. Paraprofessional*

151

Present Level of Performance

Include these IEP Team considerations for IEP development:

- The strengths of the student.
- The concerns of the parents/guardian for enhancing the education of the youth.
- For students age 14 and older, consider the student's preferences, needs, interests, and post-school outcomes.

The *Present Level* statements must identify how the student's disability affects involvement and progress in general education.

Family and Student Vision:

Ethan's goal for himself is to do well in school. He states that he "would like to get in trouble less often and be able to focus on my schoolwork so that I can do my best." Mr. & Mrs. Smith's goal for Ethan is for him to do well in school both behaviorally and academically.

Strengths of the Child and Concerns of the Parents/Guardian for Enhancing Education:

Ethan has a good sense of humor. He can be very pleasant and often initiates greetings and conversation with adults and peers. Ethan also responds well to praise. He enjoys being the classroom helper and does well when assigned specific tasks. He is a strong reader and comprehends very well. He excels in sports and participates on the school basketball and football teams.

Ethan needs to continue to improve his ability to follow instructions. He also needs to improve his on-task behavior and task completion. Ethan continues to struggle with talking out and making random noises in class. Due to Ethan's disruptive behaviors, he has occasional peer problems.

Ethan needs to improve his academic performance across all subject areas. Due to frequent off-task behavior, Ethan is not completing in-class assignments. He also is having trouble completing and turning in homework assignments. Ethan has difficulty following instructions, which is evidenced by inaccurate completion of in-school work and tests. These behaviors have had a significant and negative effect on Ethan's grades.

Present Level of Performance:

Ethan has difficulty staying focused in class. He often fidgets, daydreams, and blurts out. He has difficulty following instructions, maintaining on-task behavior, and completing work. According to the WIAT-II (Wechsler Individual Achievement Test, Second Edition), Ethan is functioning at or above grade level in all academic areas. These test scores imply that he is cognitively capable of the work currently being assigned. Currently, Ethan is participating in the Boys Town Social Skills Curriculum to remediate his behaviors and allow him to reach his expected potential in the classroom.

Least-Restrictive Environment

Appropriate Education in the Least-Restrictive Environment. Consider accommodation, modification, adaptations, assistive technology, and supplementary aids and services. What does the student require to be successful and to be educated to the maximum extent appropriate with non-disabled peers? What supports do teachers or other personnel need to assist in making this student successful in the classroom?

In the present setting, Ethan is able to participate in all general education classes. Ethan needs behavioral modifications and accommodations in order to ensure success within this environment. He will be more successful with a small student-to-teacher ratio, use of the Boys Town Social Skills Curriculum, and small-group instruction that can enable him to participate in the regular education classroom. This is currently possible using co-teaching methods. If educational placement should change, this should be reviewed.

Special Considerations:
(check areas that apply and address these in the appropriate areas of the IEP)

☒ A. If behavior impedes learning, consideration of appropriate behavioral strategies.

☐ B. If English proficiency is limited, consideration of language needs.

☐ C. If blind or visually impaired, consideration of need for braille instruction.

☐ D. If deaf or hard of hearing, consideration of the student's communication needs.

☐ E. Consideration of student's need for assistive technology service or device.

☐ F. Consideration of student's health needs.
(Attach Related Health Service Plan, if appropriate.)

☐ G. Consideration of transition services for students age 14 or older.
(Attach TRANSITION PLAN.)

Participation in Assessments:

☐ The child will participate in district-wide assessments:
  ☐ without modification
  ☒ with modification, as specified
  Small group with extended time offered, frequent breaks, and prompts as needed.

☐ The child will participate in the alternate assessment.

Participation in Physical Education:

☒ This child will participate in regular Physical Education.

☐ This child will participate in special Physical Education; see IEP goal(s).

☐ This child will participate in a modified Physical Education.

Modified PE Description:

Services/Progress Reporting

Description of Special Education Services: instructional, support, and related services

Service	Time and Frequency	Setting for Services		
Social Skills Curriculum	100%	☒ General Ed	☒ SpEd	
Small staff-to-student ratio	100%	☒ General Ed	☒ SpEd	
Small-group instruction	As needed	☒ General Ed	☒ SpEd	
		☐ General Ed	☐ SpEd	
		☐ General Ed	☐ SpEd	

*Attached Checklist will detail modifications/accommodations

Description of Special Education Service Delivery:

☐ No ☒ Yes   Are specialized transportation services required? If yes, describe:

Setting Consideration: Consider any potential harmful effects of the selected settings or to the quality of services received.

Options considered:
None noted

REMOVAL FROM GENERAL EDUCATION   _0_ %.

How would providing special education services and activities in the general education classroom impact this student?
Placing Ethan in a co-teaching classroom provides the benefits of peer models for appropriate behavior. In a classroom with low student-to-staff ratio and a small population, Ethan can get the attention he needs to help him develop the social skills required for success in a regular education classroom.

How would providing special education services and activities in the general education environment impact other students?
Ethan's off-task and blurting-out behaviors can distract other students from their studies. His behavioral needs might monopolize the teacher's time. Ethan would be disruptive to a regular education classroom that did not offer special education services.

You will be informed of your child's progress _4_ times per year.
You will receive:

☐ An IEP report at least every 90 days.
☒ Updated copies of the goal pages.

An additional page should be used for each goal, and goals for transition services can be recorded on this page.

Baseline: Ethan is on task 20% of the time on an average day.

Measurable Annual Goal: By February 20XX, Ethan will increase his on-task time to at least 70% on average. Kathy Wong will measure this by no fewer than three, 30-minute time sample behavioral observations during different classes and times of the day.

Short-Term Objectives or Benchmarks

(Each objective or benchmark should be related to enabling the youth to be involved in or progress in the general curriculum, and should be related to meeting each of the youth's other needs.)

1. Ethan will use the steps of *Staying on Task* described in the school's Social Skills Curriculum.
2. Ethan will use the steps of *Ignoring Distractions* described in the school's Social Skills Curriculum.
3. Ethan will use the steps of *Working Independently* described in the school's Social Skills Curriculum.

Progress Report

Schedule	(I) Evaluation Procedures	(II) Progress (date of review)				(III) Is progress sufficient to achieve annual goal?			
Quarterly		Initials	Initials	Initials	Initials	Initials	Initials	Initials	Initials
		Date	Date	Date	Date	Date	Date	Date	Date
		Code	Code	Code	Code	Code	Code	Code	Code

Person(s) responsible for above goal:

Comments on student progress in meeting the goals or objectives/benchmarks:

Statement of how student's progress will be reported to parents (i.e., progress reports, letters, phone calls, etc.):

Progress Report Codes

(I) Evaluation Procedures/Instruments
- A. Teacher Observation
- B. Written Performance
- C. Oral Performance
- D. Criterion Reference Test
- E. Guardian
- F. Parent Report
- G. Time Sample
- H. Report Card
- I. Point Card
- J. Other

(II) Progress Measurement
- A. Goal Met
- B. Progress Made, Goal Not Met
- C. Little or No Progress
- D. Goal Not Addressed

(III) Is progress sufficient to achieve annual goal?
- A. Yes
- B. No

An additional page should be used for each goal, and goals for transition services can be recorded on this page.

Baseline: Ethan completes homework an average of 1 out of 5 school days.

Measurable Annual Goal: By February 20XX, Ethan will complete homework 5 out of 5 school days. This will be measured by a daily homework completion report built into the school/home note. Teachers will check "Yes" or "No" for homework completion. This data will be compiled on a weekly basis by Olivia Sanchez.

Short-Term Objectives or Benchmarks
(Each objective or benchmark should be related to enabling the youth to be involved in or progress in the general curriculum, and should be related to meeting each of the youth's other needs.)

1. Ethan will use the steps of *Completing Homework* described in the school's Social Skills Curriculum.
2. Ethan will write all homework assignments down and use a binder to organize his materials 100% of the time.
3. Ethan will use the steps of *Asking for Help* described in the school's Social Skills Curriculum.
4. Ethan will use the steps of *Using Study Skills* described in the school's Social Skills Curriculum.

Progress Report

Schedule	(I) Evaluation Procedures	(II) Progress (date of review)				(III) Is progress sufficient to achieve annual goal?			
Quarterly		Initials	Initials	Initials	Initials	Initials	Initials	Initials	Initials
		Date	Date	Date	Date	Date	Date	Date	Date
		Code	Code	Code	Code	Code	Code	Code	Code

Person(s) responsible for above goal:

Comments on student progress in meeting the goals or objectives/benchmarks:

Statement of how student's progress will be reported to parents (i.e., progress reports, letters, phone calls, etc.):

Progress Report Codes

(I) **Evaluation Procedures/Instruments**
A. Teacher Observation
B. Written Performance
C. Oral Performance
D. Criterion Reference Test
E. Guardian
F. Parent Report
G. Time Sample
H. Report Card
I. Point Card
J. Other

(II) **Progress Measurement**
A. Goal Met
B. Progress Made, Goal Not Met
C. Little or No Progress
D. Goal Not Addressed

(III) **Is progress sufficient to achieve annual goal?**
A. Yes
B. No

156

An additional page should be used for each goal, and goals for transition services can be recorded on this page.

Baseline: Ethan completes 60% of tasks.

Measurable Annual Goal: Ethan will complete 90% of tasks as measured by his daily behavior report card that is built into the school/home note. Teachers will list ratio of assignments completed (e.g., 4/5). This data will be compiled on a weekly basis by Olivia Sanchez.

Short-Term Objectives or Benchmarks

(Each objective or benchmark should be related to enabling the youth to be involved in or progress in the general curriculum, and should be related to meeting each of the youth's other needs.)

1. Ethan will use the steps of *Completing Tasks* described in the school's Social Skills Curriculum.
2. Ethan will use the steps of *Checking In (or Checking Back)* described in the school's Social Skills Curriculum.
3. Ethan will use the steps of *Persevering on Tasks and Projects* described in the school's Social Skills Curriculum.

Progress Report

Schedule	(I) Evaluation Procedures	(II) Progress (date of review)				(III) Is progress sufficient to achieve annual goal?			
Quarterly		Initials	Initials	Initials	Initials	Initials	Initials	Initials	Initials
		Date	Date	Date	Date	Date	Date	Date	Date
		Code	Code	Code	Code	Code	Code	Code	Code

Person(s) responsible for above goal:

Comments on student progress in meeting the goals or objectives/benchmarks:

Statement of how student's progress will be reported to parents (i.e., progress reports, letters, phone calls, etc.):

Progress Report Codes

(I) Evaluation Procedures/Instruments
- A. Teacher Observation
- B. Written Performance
- C. Oral Performance
- D. Criterion Reference Test
- E. Guardian
- F. Parent Report
- G. Time Sample
- H. Report Card
- I. Point Card
- J. Other

(II) Progress Measurement
- A. Goal Met
- B. Progress Made, Goal Not Met
- C. Little or No Progress
- D. Goal Not Addressed

(III) Is progress sufficient to achieve annual goal?
- A. Yes
- B. No

An additional page should be used for each goal, and goals for transition services can be recorded on this page.

Baseline: Ethan follows 40% of instructions given on an average day.

Measurable Annual Goal: Ethan will increase instructions followed to at least 70% on average as measured by his daily behavior report card built into the school/home note. Teachers will list the ratio of instructions followed (e.g., 8/10). This data will be compiled weekly by Olivia Sanchez.

Short-Term Objectives or Benchmarks

(Each objective or benchmark should be related to enabling the youth to be involved in or progress in the general curriculum, and should be related to meeting each of the youth's other needs.)

1. Ethan will use the steps of *Following Instructions* described in the school's Social Skills Curriculum.
2. Ethan will use the steps of *Following Written Instructions* described in the school's Social Skills Curriculum.

Progress Report

Schedule	(I) Evaluation Procedures	(II) Progress (date of review)				(III) Is progress sufficient to achieve annual goal?			
Quarterly		Initials	Initials	Initials	Initials	Initials	Initials	Initials	Initials
		Date	Date	Date	Date	Date	Date	Date	Date
		Code	Code	Code	Code	Code	Code	Code	Code

Person(s) responsible for above goal:

Comments on student progress in meeting the goals or objectives/benchmarks:

Statement of how student's progress will be reported to parents (i.e., progress reports, letters, phone calls, etc.):

Progress Report Codes

(I) Evaluation Procedures/Instruments
- A. Teacher Observation
- B. Written Performance
- C. Oral Performance
- D. Criterion Reference Test
- E. Guardian
- F. Parent Report
- G. Time Sample
- H. Report Card
- I. Point Card
- J. Other

(II) Progress Measurement
- A. Goal Met
- B. Progress Made, Goal Not Met
- C. Little or No Progress
- D. Goal Not Addressed

(III) Is progress sufficient to achieve annual goal?
- A. Yes
- B. No

An additional page should be used for each goal, and goals for transition services can be recorded on this page.

Baseline: Ethan blurts out and makes unsolicited noises about 20 times a day.

Measurable Annual Goal: Ethan will blurt out and make unsolicited noises no more than 5 times a day. Ethan will self-monitor his blurting-out and noise-making behavior by using a written log. The log will be checked by the teacher at the end of each period. At that time, the teacher will mark whether they agree or disagree with Ethan's self-assessment, providing observations if necessary. This data will be compiled by Sean Harmon (guidance counselor) and reviewed with Ethan on a weekly basis.

Short-Term Objectives or Benchmarks

(Each objective or benchmark should be related to enabling the youth to be involved in or progress in the general curriculum, and should be related to meeting each of the youth's other needs.)

1. Ethan will use the steps of *Getting Another Person's Attention* described in the school's Social Skills Curriculum.
2. Ethan will use the steps of *Getting the Teacher's Attention* described in the school's Social Skills Curriculum.
3. Ethan will use the steps of *Interrupting Appropriately* described in the school's Social Skills Curriculum.
4. Ethan will use the steps of *Self-Correcting Your Own Behaviors* described in the school's Social Skills Curriculum.

Progress Report

Schedule	(I) Evaluation Procedures	(II) Progress (date of review)				(III) Is progress sufficient to achieve annual goal?			
Quarterly		Initials	Initials	Initials	Initials	Initials	Initials	Initials	Initials
		Date	Date	Date	Date	Date	Date	Date	Date
		Code	Code	Code	Code	Code	Code	Code	Code

Person(s) responsible for above goal:

Comments on student progress in meeting the goals or objectives/benchmarks:

Statement of how student's progress will be reported to parents (i.e., progress reports, letters, phone calls, etc.):

Progress Report Codes

(I) Evaluation Procedures/Instruments
  A. Teacher Observation
  B. Written Performance
  C. Oral Performance
  D. Criterion Reference Test
  E. Guardian
  F. Parent Report
  G. Time Sample
  H. Report Card
  I. Point Card
  J. Other

(II) Progress Measurement
  A. Goal Met
  B. Progress Made, Goal Not Met
  C. Little or No Progress
  D. Goal Not Addressed

(III) Is progress sufficient to achieve annual goal?
  A. Yes
  B. No

159

Transition

Ethan is only 11 years old and doesn't require a transition plan at this time.

_____ Beginning at age 14 (or younger, if appropriate), updated annually, a statement of the child's transition services, focusing on their course of study.

_____
_____
_____

_____ Beginning at age 16 (or younger, if appropriate), updated annually, a statement of needed transition services (indicate the strengths and/or needs for each area):

Instruction: _____

Related Services: _____

Community Experiences: _____

Development of Employment and Other Post-School Options: _____

Daily Living Skills: _____

Functional Vocational Evaluation: _____

Interagency Linkages and Responsibilities: _____

Transition Activities	Agency Responsible	Date

Anticipated graduation date: _____ (must be provided at least 18 months prior to graduation)

Notice of transfer of rights provided:

Transfer of rights will occur at age _____. Date:

Accommodations of Methods and Materials

- ☒ Provide support and cueing system
- ☐ Use mnemonic devices
- ☐ Use visual and graphic representations
- ☒ Provide written notes and outlines
- ☒ Highlight important concepts
- ☒ Repeat key material
- ☒ Increase hands-on, concrete learning experiences
- ☐ Use alternative methods of providing information
- ☒ Break lesson into smaller segments
- ☐ Allow use of tape recorders or devices
- ☐ Other_____

Accommodations of Assignments and Assessments

- ☐ Provide assistance and support in advance
- ☐ Allow alternate formats and response modes
- ☒ Provide ongoing coaching and feedback
- ☐ Allow recorder or word processor
- ☐ Allow oral responses
- ☐ Use blocked assignments on worksheets
- ☒ Divide worksheets into segments
- ☐ Use folders for storing assignments
- ☐ Use assistive technology
- ☐ Use alternatives for written assignments
- ☐ Increase or decrease the amount of practice
- ☐ Modify homework assignments
- ☒ Provide extra time to complete assignments or tests
- ☒ Break up test administration to shorter sessions
- ☐ Test orally
- ☒ Allow writing on test (vs. other sheet)
- ☐ Other_____

Accommodations to the Learning Environment

- ☐ Modify the physical setting
- ☒ Use study carrels or proximity seating
- ☒ Modify grouping arrangements
- ☐ Provide guidance and assistance on tasks
- ☐ Use small-group instruction
- ☐ Provide peer tutoring
- ☒ Modify classroom management procedures
- ☒ Use specialized behavior management procedures
- ☒ Implement daily or weekly reporting to parents
- ☒ Use checklists, notebooks, or other on-task aides
- ☐ Use time-specific assignments
- ☐ Other_____

- ☐ NO ACCOMMODATIONS NEEDED

LELAND: Bold, Determined Maverick and Independent Spirit with the Drive to Become a Strong Leader

Synopsis: Leland is a twelve-year-old boy who has been evaluated by a licensed mental health professional and diagnosed with Oppositional Defiant Disorder (ODD). Symptoms, present for more than a year, are resulting in significant problems at school, home, and in the community. The diagnosis was based on multiple sources of information, including clinically elevated DISC scores for ODD; clinically significant scores on the ASEBA Child Behavior Checklist Parent Form and ASEBA Teacher Report Form on both the Aggressive Behavior syndrome subscale and ODD DSM-oriented subscale; and biological parent and Family-Teacher (primary caregiver) reports of the following DSM-5 diagnostic criteria:

- Often loses temper.

- Regularly argues with adults.

- Often defies or refuses to comply with adults' requests or rules.

- Blames others for mistakes and misbehavior.

- Deliberately annoys others and is spiteful and vindictive.

Artifact Samples Below:

- Voicemail transcript from mom to the residential group home program

- Copy of the *Family Preservation Remedial Services Individualized Treatment Plan*

>>> VOICEMAIL TRANSCRIPT FROM MOM

"Hi Boys Town Team,

"I just want to express my gratitude for your willingness to help Leland. His sister and I have been extremely worried about him for a while now, given the abandonment he feels from his dad leaving, the trauma he has experienced in his young life, and because of the troublesome 'friends' he has made (after losing friends who were more positive influences in his life because of his vindictiveness and anger) to fill those voids and to ease the pain he has felt from trying to cope with our struggles. Tanisha, his sister, and I have tried so hard to set him down the right path, but it feels like we lose Leland a little more each day. He just seems to get more and more angry. He won't help out at home, lies, blames others for his own actions, argues and yells when anyone tries to set rules, purposefully breaks any rules that are set, and even curses and gets verbally aggressive! It's Leland's way or NO way, in his mind. I just don't know how else to help him when he won't even respect or listen to me.

"If you'd like, I can get you in touch with his teachers, too. I've been walking on eggshells daily, just waiting for that call telling me he disrespected a teacher or faculty member, wronged a classmate, or he was sent to the office again. His grades have dropped so rapidly, his teachers are unsure how to support him in raising his GPA because he simply will not put in the effort or even listen to them!

"The straw that broke the camel's back though was the situation with a security guard. He and a friend matched the description of two other boys who stole from the neighborhood store. When a security guard questioned him, Leland threatened him!

"We have been in outpatient therapy together for SIX MONTHS now, and it's such a struggle. He won't do the work, doesn't seem to even care about the struggle and pain he is causing. He flat out refuses to engage. I just want my little boy to be happy. To find ways to cope with all of the hardballs we've been dealt, to gain the confidence to make better choices, and to be a productive member of society. I hope you can help us make that dream come true. Thanks."

Individualized Treatment Plan
Family Home Program

NAME: Leland Jackson	**REPORT PERIOD FROM:** 3/2/20XX	**TO:** 3/31/20XX
BOYS TOWN ID#: 1234567	**ADMIT DATE:** 2/17/20XX	
MEDICAID ID#: 123-45-6789-10	**GENDER:** Male	
AGE: 12	**DOB:** 01/10/XXXX	**GRADE:** 7th
FAMILY-TEACHERS: Tom & Jane Hopkins	**ADDRESS:** 12345 Farm Circle, City, ST 68010 **PHONE NUMBER:** 555-123-4567	
LEGAL GUARDIAN: Mark Cobb	**ADDRESS:** 12345 Dodge Street, City, ST 68111 **PHONE NUMBER:** 555-333-4567	
ATTENDING PHYSICIAN: Dr. Joseph Wright	**THERAPIST:** Carla Peterson, M.S.	
CLINICAL SPECIALIST: Michael Hill	**MOTIVATION SYSTEM:** Daily	

DIAGNOSIS

313.81 Oppositional Defiant Disorder
Moderate-to-severe environmental stressors. Early physical abuse and neglect, multiple out-of-home placements, ward of the state of Nebraska, uninvolved biological father

Treatment Progress/Update

GOAL #1: Leland will learn to respect authority in all environments, including home and school.

Obj. #	Objective	Estimated Target Date	Open/ Closed	Level of Progress			
				A	P	MP	NP
1.1	Leland will learn the skill of *Accepting Criticism* by earning fewer than "2" concerns daily.	6/1/20XX	OPEN		X		
1.2	Leland will learn the skill of *Accepting Decisions of Authority* by earning "1" or fewer concerns daily.	6/1/20XX	OPEN		X		
1.3	Leland will *Follow Rules* at school, earning fewer than "2" concerns daily and "0" homework concerns.	6/1/20XX	OPEN		X		

KEY: Denotes Level of Progress on Objective: **A**=Achieved/Generalized; **P**=Progress Made; **MP**=Minimal Progress Made; **NP**=No Progress

Current Review Period: _____ 3/2/20XX _____ To _____ 3/31/20XX _____

In regard to learning to respect authority, Leland has made progress in all of his objectives. Leland regularly accepts criticism/feedback from Family-Teachers, schoolteachers, and peers. Leland earned concerns for accepting criticism/feedback on 3/7, 3/13, 3/15, 3/21, 3/22, and 3/29. Leland has complained, rolled his eyes, argued, and made noises instead of accepting criticism/feedback.

Leland continues to show progress with accepting decisions by not arguing. He earned concerns on 3/8, 3/11, 3/15, 3/16, and 3/24. The majority of these were for not completing his chores and doing his laundry.

Leland has been able to follow the rules at school. He has not earned an office referral and has been able to earn less than "2" concerns each day with the exception of one day. Leland struggled in class on 3/18. He interrupted his teacher and spoke out of turn. He received an office referral warning for disrupting the class. Leland showed acceptance by decreasing his disruptive behavior and not arguing.

GOAL #2: Leland will develop his communication and interaction skills.

Obj. #	Objective	Estimated Target Date	Open/ Closed	Level of Progress			
				A	P	MP	NP
2.1	Leland will learn the skill of *Using an Appropriate Voice Tone (or Level)* when interacting with others, earning "1" or fewer negative consequences per day.	8/1/20XX	OPEN			X	
2.2	Leland will learn to engage in appropriate conversations with his peers, earning at least "1" positive daily for using the skill of *Choosing Appropriate Words*.	8/1/20XX	OPEN			X	

KEY: Denotes Level of Progress on Objective: **A**=Achieved/Generalized; **P**=Progress Made; **MP**=Minimal Progress Made; **NP**=No Progress

Current Review Period: _____3/2/20XX_____ To _____3/31/20XX_____

Leland has displayed minimal progress in using an appropriate voice tone and volume. He earned concerns on 3/12 for laughing at his peers and speaking over them. On 3/13, Leland used sarcastic voice tones when speaking to his peers. On 3/17, Leland earned concerns for blurting out answers and yelling in the house. On 3/29, Leland used a rude voice tone with both his peers and adults.

Leland has displayed improvements in choosing appropriate words during conversations with others. He struggles with maintaining a conversation, making positive comments, and not interrupting. Leland earned concerns for inappropriate topics and rude language in conversations on 3/3, 3/7, 3/13, 3/16, 3/17, 3/18, 3/22, 3/23, 3/24, and 3/29.

GOAL #3: Leland will learn to manage his feelings and emotions appropriately.

Obj. #	Objective	Estimated Target Date	Open/ Closed	Level of Progress			
				A	P	MP	NP
3.1	Leland will learn the skill of *Using Anger Control Strategies*, earning one positive per day.	5/1/20XX	OPEN			X	
3.2	Leland will use his self-control skills when *Dealing with Frustration*, earning "1" or fewer consequences per day.	5/1/20XX	OPEN		X		
3.3	Leland will learn the skill of *Expressing Feelings Appropriately*, earning one positive per day.	5/1/20XX	OPEN			X	

KEY: Denotes Level of Progress on Objective: **A**=Achieved/Generalized; **P**=Progress Made; **MP**=Minimal Progress Made; **NP**=No Progress

Current Review Period:_____3/2/20XX_____ To_____3/31/20XX_____

Concerning the skill of *Using Anger Control Strategies,* Leland has made minimal progress. Leland earned positives for using this skill only 10 out of 30 days: 3/5, 3/7, 3/11, 3/13, 3/15, 3/18, 3/20, 3/21, 3/22, and 3/31. On other occasions, he typically chooses to "shut down" rather than use his anger control strategies.

Leland has made progress in using the skill of *Dealing with Frustrations* by having one instance of crying on 3/4. This was brought on by a last-minute notification that his mother would not be visiting him on a weekend as planned. He has had no incidents of aggression.

Leland has made minimal progress with expressing his feelings appropriately. He was able to express his feelings about his mother not making family therapy, not being able to participate in Boy Scouts, and his sister not calling for a few weeks. After Leland expressed his feelings, he quickly moved on. When he was disappointed about not seeing his mother on the weekend, he wrote her a letter. When he found out he couldn't participate in Boy Scouts, he decided to make some new friends, and he has become active by participating in community functions, playing outside, initiating games, and getting involved in school activities. When his sister was on vacation, he was able to write her a card and then go outside to play. While these are healthy coping strategies, Leland also needs to continue working on verbally expressing his feelings to others.

Non-Prioritized Goals

Goal #	Goal Description	Level of Progress			
		A	P	MP	NP
4	Leland will learn independent living skills.		X		
5	Leland will improve his relationships with his family.		X		
6	Leland will develop his academic skills.		X		

In regard to Leland's non-prioritized goals, he has made progress in all areas. Leland has improved his hygiene by showering, brushing his teeth, and cleaning his room on a daily basis. He also has participated in the self-government process in the home by being elected manager of the home by his peers.

Leland has made efforts to improve his relationship with both his mother and his caseworker. He has been able to work on his relationship with his caseworker, Tonya, by speaking to her on a regular basis and sending her letters bi-weekly. Leland has discussed his progress with his mother and continues to ask how she is doing.

Academically, Leland was able to participate in class on a regular basis. Leland's teachers reported that he was pleasant to have in class and that he displayed good quality work on his assignments. Leland finished the fourth quarter with a 3.0 GPA. Leland did not miss a day of school, earning only 2 tardies for the semester.

TREATMENT STRATEGIES: Family-Teachers will target social skills in areas where Leland is deficient. Family-Teachers will do role-plays and complete daily skill review sheets each day. Family-Teachers will make sure that Leland has appropriate prosocial activities to engage in with his peers. Family-Teachers will check Leland's homework each night for completion and check his organizational skills. Family-Teachers will use the SODAS (Situation, Options, Disadvantages, Advantages, Solution) method with Leland to help him solve problems and critically think through important school, peer, and personal issues. Family-Teachers will use self-government meetings to promote accepting and giving feedback, as well as problem solving. Family-Teachers will have Leland set daily goals for himself and teach appropriate conversation and friendship skills to Leland.

LEGAL AND AGENCY INVOLVEMENT: Leland is a state ward. His case manager is Tonya Thompson. She can be reached at 555-321-4567. He also has a guardian ad litem (GAL), Mark Cobb.

ASSESSMENT ACTIVITY: Ongoing academic assessment, therapeutic assessment, medication review, direct observation, in-home observation, weekly consultation, and card reviews will be conducted to assess Leland's progress in the Family Home Program.

Responsible Parties (Modalities)					
Medical Professional (as needed)	X	Health Care Coordinator (as needed)		Specialized Religious Education (as needed)	
Psychiatric Professional (monthly)	X	Nutritionist (as needed)		Chemical Dependency Services (as needed)	
Medications (daily as needed)	X	Common Sense Parenting® (weekly)		Other	
Specialized Clinical Services (weekly)	X	Specialized Family Services (as needed)	X		
Specialized Educational Services (daily)	X	Family Home Program (daily)	X		

Medical Information	
CURRENT MEDICATIONS: Leland is currently off all psychotropic medications.	**PAST MEDICATIONS:** Depakote, DDAVP, Zyprexa, Ferrous Sulphate, Clonidine, Dexedrine, Imipramine, Risperdal
MEDICAL APPOINTMENTS/CONSULTATIONS: 3/12/20XX - Dental with Dr. Mayer (sealants needed)	
HEIGHT: 65 inches	**WEIGHT:** 109
LAST PHYSICAL/PHYSICIAN: 1/6/20XX Dr. Robins	**LAST DENTAL/DENTIST:** 3/12/20XX Dr. Mayer
MENTAL HEALTH APPOINTMENTS/CONSULTATIONS: 3/13/20XX – individual therapy 3/29/20XX – Leland had a treatment team meeting with Dr. Wright.	

Family Work			
STRENGTHS: Leland's mother has recently become more involved in his life. Currently, she has supervised calls and therapeutic visitation with Leland. Contact with Leland's father is limited to letter writing, per Leland's request. Leland also has an older sister, Tanisha, who has been a consistent adult in his life the last few years.			

	Goals	Completed	Not Completed	Ongoing
1.	Leland and his mother will attend family therapy regularly.			X
2.	Leland and his mother will work on communication skills by talking on the phone on a regular basis. This will be monitored by one of the Hopkins' team members.			X
3.	Leland will express his feelings about his father, if he receives letters or chooses to write a letter to his father.			X
4.	Leland will maintain appropriate contact with his sister, Tanisha Jackson.			X

FAMILY PATHWAY: None/Minimal Contact.

FAMILY CONTACT: 3/11/20XX - Leland called his mother on her birthday.
3/11/20XX - Leland sent a letter to both his caseworker and his mother.
3/12/20XX - Family therapy cancelled due to transportation conflict.
3/19/20XX - Leland sent letters to his mother, his caseworker, and his sister.

FAMILY THERAPY: Leland was scheduled for family therapy on 3/12/20XX. Family therapy did not occur due to transportation concerns and his mother not being able to attend the therapy session.

Discharge Plan Review:

REFERRAL BEHAVIORS: Verbal and physical aggression, out of instructional control, poor social skills, poor coping skills, peer relation concerns, arguing, dishonesty, poor hygiene, and low self-esteem.

PROGRESS MADE: Leland has been able to make new friends in the community, and he interacts by playing games, riding bikes, and hanging out with his friends on a daily basis. Leland has shown improvement with decreasing his arguing and by improving his personal hygiene.

ESTIMATED LENGTH OF STAY & DISCHARGE PLAN: Leland will remain at Home Campus until treatment goals can be reached, with an anticipated discharge date of January 20XX. Discharge plan is a foster care setting. Permanency plan will likely be the state foster care system.

BARRIERS TO TREATMENT: Leland is socially awkward and could struggle with being teased at school. Leland has difficulty coping with family issues, and family contact is very limited at this time.

Review Dates	
INITIAL REVIEW:	2/17/20XX-3/1/20XX
REVIEW #2:	3/2/20XX-3/31/20XX
REVIEW #3:	
REVIEW #4:	
REVIEW #5:	
REVIEW #6:	
NEXT REVIEW DATE:	4/30/20XX

How satisfied are you with the progress you have made over this report period?

_____
Youth Signature

Signatures

1. NAME:_____

TITLE: _____

DATE: _____

☐ Present   ☐ Conf call   ☐ Did not attend
_____

2. NAME:_____

TITLE: _____

DATE: _____

☐ Present   ☐ Conf call   ☐ Did not attend
_____

3. NAME:_____

TITLE: _____

DATE: _____

☐ Present   ☐ Conf call   ☐ Did not attend
_____

4. NAME:_____

TITLE: _____

DATE: _____

☐ Present   ☐ Conf call   ☐ Did not attend
_____

5. NAME:_____

TITLE: _____

DATE: _____

☐ Present   ☐ Conf call   ☐ Did not attend
_____

6. NAME:_____

TITLE: _____

DATE: _____

☐ Present   ☐ Conf call   ☐ Did not attend
_____

7. NAME:_____

TITLE: _____

DATE: _____

☐ Present   ☐ Conf call   ☐ Did not attend
_____

8. NAME:_____

TITLE: _____

DATE: _____

☐ Present   ☐ Conf call   ☐ Did not attend
_____

I have reviewed the attached treatment plan and approve its contents.

_____   _____

Joseph E. Wright, M.D.   date

IYLA: Introspective, Insightful, and Looking for a Way to See Glimmers of Light in Moments of Darkness

Synopsis: Iyla is a thirteen-year-old girl who has been evaluated by a psychiatrist and diagnosed with Major Depressive Disorder, Recurrent, Severe. Symptoms are resulting in significant problems at school, at home, and with friends. The diagnosis was based on multiple sources of information, including clinically elevated DISC scores for Major Depressive Disorder; clinically significant scores on the ASEBA Child Behavior Checklist Parent Form, ASEBA Teacher Report Form, and ASEBA Youth Report Form on both the Withdrawn/Depressed syndrome subscale and Affective problems DSM-oriented subscale; and biological parent and teacher reports and therapist observation of the following DSM-5 diagnostic criteria:

- Two suicide attempts in the last twelve months.
- Depressed mood most of the day, most every day.
- Diminished interest in daily activities and previously pleasurable activities.
- Significant weight loss.
- Insomnia.
- Feelings of worthlessness.
- Diminished ability to think or concentrate.
- Fatigue and loss of energy.

Artifact Samples Below:

- Diary entry that Iyla shared with her psychologist, which led to a team decision to place Iyla in a residential psychiatric center for youth
- Copy of the *Intensive Residential Treatment Center Comprehensive Treatment Plan*

>>> EXCERPT FROM IYLA'S DIARY

Dear Diary,

I can't take it anymore. I like, don't even know why I'm here. In and out of inpatient care, still in outpatient and seeing a psych regularly, a team of doctors always on my back, my parents are worried sick and for what? Why do they care so much? I suck at everything I do and I know I must be such a disappointment to them. They always tell me they love me, they show me pictures of the girl I used to be, back when I was happy and cared and wasn't trapped in this feeling of grey and they say that they want the "Old Iyla" back. I hear my mom crying at night. I see the pain on my dad's face when he tries to get me to do the things we used to love like movie night and pancake Sunday and weekend bike rides and I just tell him to GO AWAY but, I'm so just tired and worthless and nothing makes me happy anymore. Not even drama club and I used to LOVE drama club. My theater friends still text and stuff, trying to get me to go to practice but I just can't. I am too tired and just want to be alone. Besides, I know I'll screw up my lines or something and let everyone down. Typical stupid Iyla, right? I'll bet that's what they would think. I mean heck, I know my teacher must already think that, too! I'm like, failing my classes or something now. Which is weird because I used to make the honor roll every quarter, but I just can't concentrate in class and I don't care enough to do the work. Maybe it's because I'm so tired. I can't eat because my stomach is always wrenched in sadness and I can't sleep because...well, I don't know why but I just can't bring myself to get a good night's sleep. Like I even deserve one, right? I'm so sick of feeling nothing but sad or numbness and so sick of being a failure. Last week, I cut my legs with a razor blade just to feel SOMETHING and to punish myself for being this way. It's not enough though. It didn't help. Nothing helps. Which is why I have a plan. Maybe once I'm no longer living, my parents won't have to deal with me anymore. Maybe I won't be such a burden on everyone. Maybe I will finally get out of this feeling I'm trapped in. Maybe.

Goodnight, Diary. You're the only one who understands.

Forever yours,

Iyla

Intensive Residential Treatment Center
Comprehensive Treatment Plan

NAME: Iyla Jones		**D.O.B.:** 12/26/1995
MEDICAL RECORD #: 123-4567-89		
Review Dates		
ADMISSION DATE: 10/13/XX	**INITIAL TX PLAN:** 10/28/XX	
REVIEW #1: 11/12/XX	**REVIEW #2:**	
REVIEW #3:	**REVIEW #4:**	
REVIEW #5:	**REVIEW #6:**	
REVIEW #7:	**REVIEW #8:**	
DATE OF NEXT TREATMENT REVIEW: November 27, 20XX		

CURRENT DIAGNOSIS (Updated: 06/09/XX by Joseph Wright, M.D.)

296.90 Major Depressive Disorder, Recurrent, Severe, No Psychosis
307.42 Insomnia-Maintaining Sleep related to Major Depressive Disorder, Recurrent, Severe, No Psychosis
History of 296.90 Mood Disorder, Unspecified
Moderate environmental stressors including several inpatient stays and long-time best friend moved away

ADMISSION MEDICATIONS: Seroquel 25mg in p.m., Prozac 20mg daily, Abilify 10mg daily

STRENGTHS: Iyla is intelligent, attractive, polite, kind, and likable.

INTENSIVE RESIDENTIAL TREATMENT CENTER (IRTC) TREATMENT TEAM MEMBERS: Joseph Wright, M.D.; Juan Gonzalez, Program Director; Carla Peterson, M.S., Therapist; Joan Kemp, Educational Therapist; IRTC Nursing Staff; Mike Shaw, IRTC Unit Coordinator; Jackson Sheppard, IRTC Shift Manager; IRTC Behavioral Health Technicians.

Priority Yes	No	Assessment	Date Identified	Problem List
X		X	10/28/XX	1. Depressed and withdrawn (youth presents at time of admission with a flat affect)
X		X	10/28/XX	2. Insomnia
X			10/28/XX	3. Poor coping skills
X			10/28/XX	4. Poor problem-solving skills
X			10/28/XX	5. Difficulty appropriately expressing feelings
X			10/28/XX	6. Difficulty coping with loss
X		X	10/28/XX	7. Suicidal ideations
X			10/28/XX	8. Suicide attempts
X			10/28/XX	9. School attendance problems (refusal to attend)
X			10/28/XX	10. Peer relationship problems (youth identified that her only female friend recently moved away)
X			10/28/XX	11. Inappropriate boundaries (youth will quickly identify female peers as "friends" without consideration and will quickly become attached to male peers)
X		X	10/28/XX	12. Relationship problems within the immediate family (believes older sister is favored by her parents; parents will often criticize lyla for small mistakes)
X		X	10/28/XX	13. Self-harm behaviors (youth admits to cutting her inner thighs when upset)
X			10/28/XX	14. Refusal to participate in positive activities
X			10/28/XX	15. Decreased academic performance

*Items checked "no" require justification for lack of inclusion in treatment plan.

GOALS AND OBJECTIVES (established at Review #1)

GOAL A: lyla will learn how to appropriately cope and deal with her emotions and feelings.

Objectives	Review Period											
	1	3	5	7	9	11	13	15	17	19	21	23
1. lyla will use the skill of *Making Positive Self-Statements* a minimum of 5 times per day by 02/12/XX.	MP											
2. lyla will use the skill of *Using Structured Problem-Solving* (SODAS) a minimum of 1 time per day by 02/12/XX.	NP											
3. lyla will use the skill of *Coping with Sad Feelings* (or *Depression*) a minimum of 5 times per day by 02/12/XX.	NP											
4. lyla will use the skill of *Expressing Feelings Appropriately* a minimum of 5 times per day by 02/12/XX.	NP											
5. lyla will use the skill of *Expressing Optimism* a minimum of 5 times per day by 02/12/XX.	MP											

KEY: Denotes Level of Progress on Objective: **A**=Achieved; **P**=Progress Made; **MP**=Minimal Progress Made; **NP**=No Progress; **D**=Discontinue/No Longer Valid; **R**=Revised; **N**=New Objective; **RS**=Restart

GOAL B: Iyla will develop the ability to build positive relationships with others (relationship building).

Objectives	Review Period											
	1	3	5	7	9	11	13	15	17	19	21	23
1. Iyla will learn the skill of *Saying "No" Assertively* to increase appropriate boundaries with both male and female peers, earning no more than 1 negative consequence per week by 02/12/XX.	NP											
2. Iyla will increase her ability to build positive peer relationships. Iyla will learn the skill of *Seeking Positive Attention* from peers a minimum of 4 times per day by 02/12/XX.	MP											
3. Iyla will work on the skill of *Choosing Appropriate Friends* through individual and group therapy, which will help her build appropriate relationships that support positive behavior and build self-esteem. She will provide at least 1 example per session by 02/12/XX.	NP											
4. Iyla will learn the skill of *Making New Friends* through individual and group therapy, which will help her build appropriate relationships that support positive behavior and build self-esteem. She will provide at least 1 example per session by 02/12/XX.	MP											

KEY: Denotes Level of Progress on Objective: **A**=Achieved; **P**=Progress Made; **MP**=Minimal Progress Made; **NP**=No Progress; **D**=Discontinue/No Longer Valid; **R**=Revised; **N**=New Objective; **RS**=Restart

GOAL C: Iyla will increase participation in positive activities across environments.

Objectives	Review Period											
	1	3	5	7	9	11	13	15	17	19	21	23
1. Iyla will use the skill of *Doing Good Quality Work* across environments, earning no more than 1 negative consequence per week for poor quality work by 02/12/XX.	P											
2. Iyla will use the skill of *Participating in Activities* across environments a minimum of 4 times per day by 02/12/XX.	P											
3. Iyla will use the skill of *Showing Interest* across environments a minimum of 5 times per day by 02/12/XX.	MP											
4. Iyla will use the skill of *Contributing to Group Activities* across environments a minimum of 3 times per day by 02/12/XX.	MP											

KEY: Denotes Level of Progress on Objective: **A**=Achieved; **P**=Progress Made; **MP**=Minimal Progress Made; **NP**=No Progress; **D**=Discontinue/No Longer Valid; **R**=Revised; **N**=New Objective; **RS**=Restart

GOAL D: Iyla will participate in family therapy with her parents and sister to build a reasonable level of connectedness and trust.

Objectives	Review Period											
	1	3	5	7	9	11	13	15	17	19	21	23
1. Iyla will use the skill of *Giving Compliments* with her sister and parents in family therapy at least 3 times per session by 02/12/XX.	NP											
2. Iyla will use the skill of *Maintaining a Conversation* with her parents and sister in family therapy at least 4 times per session by 02/12/XX.	NP											
3. Iyla will use the skill of *Making Positive Statements about Others* in family therapy at least 4 times per session by 02/12/XX.	NP											

KEY: Denotes Level of Progress on Objective: **A**=Achieved; **P**=Progress Made; **MP**=Minimal Progress Made; **NP**=No Progress; **D**=Discontinue/No Longer Valid; **R**=Revised; **N**=New Objective; **RS**=Restart

Initial Treatment Plan Information

Date:_____

GOAL: Youth will undergo initial assessment in noted priority problem areas.

Objectives:

1. Collect baseline data on: Depression and withdrawal
2. Collect baseline data on: Self-harm attempts
3. Collect baseline data on: Suicidal ideation
4. Collect baseline data on: Peer interaction problems
5. Collect baseline data on: Sleep behavior
6. Collect baseline data on: Coping and problem-solving skills
7. Collect baseline data on: School performance and attendance

Restrictions: Iyla will be intensely monitored due to suicidal and self-harm behaviors. This will be assessed on a daily basis by staff and on a weekly basis by Dr. Joseph Wright.

Motivational Level System: Iyla was admitted on Level 1 privileges.

Expectations for Family/Legal Guardian Involvement: Iyla's parents, Bob and Sarah Jones, will attend family therapy two times per month. Iyla's sister, Jenna, will attend family therapy one time per month. Parents will attend monthly treatment team meetings. Family will maintain regular contact with Iyla and the therapist.

Barriers to Treatment: Previous suicide attempts and inpatient placements

Other Therapeutic and Medical Issues: Iyla will participate in individual therapy one time per week, family therapy two times per month, and treatment group therapy a minimum of two times per week. She also will participate in monthly treatment team meetings. Iyla will be able to identify her medications and the side effects.

IRTC Milieu:

Daily
- Psychotropic medications as needed
- Milieu Therapy (Boys Town Psychoeducational Model®)

Weekly
- 30-50 minutes of individual therapy
- 2-3 hours of group therapy
- 6-7 hours of recreational therapy
- A minimum of 20 hours of educational therapy

Other
- _____

Data Collection:

Daily medical chart probes, professional observation, and motivational system card data.

Reason for Continued Care and Estimated Length of Stay: Iyla was referred to the Intensive Residential Treatment Center due to other failed placements at lower levels of care (outpatient therapy, intensive outpatient therapy, and brief inpatient hospitalization). Length of stay will be based on goals achieved and maintained for a minimum of three months.

Contributing Team Members: Carla Peterson, M.S., Therapist
Absent Team Members: None

Date of Next Scheduled Treatment Review: 11/27/XX

Discharge Plan

Estimated Length of Stay from Date of Admission	• 90-120 days
Criteria for Discharge	• Will report a reduction in frequency, duration, and intensity of suicidal ideation. • Will refrain from self-harm behaviors for a minimum of 30 consecutive days. • Will display an increase in ability to utilize social and coping skills. • Will participate actively across the therapeutic milieu.
Next Projected Placement	• Partial hospitalization/Day treatment
Long-Term Placement Plan	• Home with parents, regularly attending psychiatrist and therapist appointments
Barriers to Discharge	• Difficulty maintaining stability at lower levels of care

Projected School Placement Needs:
    Date of Last IEP
    Date of Last MDT
	• Regular education
	• N/A
	• N/A

Transition	• Transitional passes will be conducted, if possible, to the next level of care to ensure a smooth transition.
Psychiatric Consultation	• Iyla would benefit from ongoing psychiatric consultation as long as she is on psychotropic medication or if any changes or discontinuations are considered.
Therapy	• Iyla would benefit from ongoing individual and family therapy.
Medical	• Routine medical intervention and physicals. Iyla will know the medication names, doses, purposes, and side effects.

Comprehensive Treatment Plan Review

Review #1 Date:_____

Behavioral Summary and Data: During the first part of this review period, we saw more suicidal ideation and self-destructive behaviors. Over the last week of the review period, we have seen more stability, though Iyla continues to struggle with utilizing problem-solving and coping skills. She tends to become withdrawn and stare off into space when upset, rather than express feelings. Iyla has endorsed suicidal ideation when speaking with her therapist and Dr. Wright on three separate occasions, resulting in three separate suicide evaluations. Iyla also must continue to focus on appropriate boundaries with male and female peers because she tries to develop friendships too quickly and becomes clingy. She also had difficulty selecting appropriate friends that would help her make positive decisions. She has involved herself in "dating" relationships with male peers. Iyla did admit that on the 13th of this month, she kissed a male peer. Sleep problems continue to be an issue, with Iyla getting up frequently throughout the night and attempting to roam the halls. It appears this is related to poor coping and problem-solving skills. The most destructive self-harm behavior occurred on 11/17/XX, when Iyla learned that one of her "best friends" was "dating" the male peer that she had kissed on the 13th. She began to scratch at her right wrist until it bled, banged her head against the wall, and pulled out some of her hair. A safety hold was required. Iyla refused to attend school on 11/18/XX, stating that she was just too tired and did not feel well. At that time, she was placed in time-out. After time-out, she was able to attend school for the rest of the day. Otherwise, Iyla has shown improvements in school performance. She is earning grades similar to those she earned before her first inpatient hospitalization. It has been noted that her few positive self-statements and expressions of optimism have been related to school performance. She has to occasionally be prompted to put forth effort, but has continued to improve over the month. Finally, only one family therapy session occurred this review period, and Iyla had difficulty exhibiting her skills in that session. She continued to complain about her parents and called her sister several names.

	Baseline Number											
	1	3	5	7	9	11	13	15	17	19	21	23
Physical Aggression	0											
Attempted Physical Assaults	0											
Physical Assaults - Adults	0											
Physical Assaults - Peers	0											
Seclusions	0											
Suicide Ideation	10											
Self-Destructive Behaviors	6											
Property Destruction	0											
Threatening Behaviors	2											
Time-Outs	2											
Safety Holds	1											

Restrictions: Iyla remains under close monitoring, which is assessed on a weekly basis by Dr. Joseph Wright.

Motivational Level System: Level 1 Privileges, Basics, ITL: Iyla earned an Intensive Treatment Level consequence on 11/17/XX when she engaged in serious self-harm behaviors.

Barriers to Treatment: Iyla has a history of difficulty maintaining stability at lower levels of care. **Additional Goal/Objective and Intervention Information (new goal areas or revisions):** Treatment goals were established during this review period to address Major Depressive Disorder and sleep concerns.

Other Therapeutic Issues Noted

Individual Therapy: Iyla's participation in individual therapy has improved as she has begun to participate more actively, complete homework, and bring topics to session.

Family Therapy: Iyla had family therapy with her parents one time during this review period. She frequently complained and was not open to her parents' feedback.

Treatment Group Therapy: Iyla's participation in treatment group therapy has varied from active and appropriate to disinterested and withdrawn.

Recreational Therapy: Iyla is participating in recreational therapy at this time with some prompting.

Current Medications: Prozac 20mg daily

Medication Changes: Seroquel and Abilify were discontinued during this review period.

Psychotropic PRNs: None

Other Medical Information:
- Height and Weight: 5'4"; 101 lbs

Date of Most Recent:
- History and Physical: 10/29/XX
- Dental Exam: see record
- Eye Exam: see record
- Immunizations: see record

Pending Medical Appointments: • None

Family/Legal Guardian Involvement: Iyla's parents participated in this month's treatment team meeting and attended family therapy one time during this review period.

Academic Status:
Review of IEP Goals and Youth Progress: No IEP; Regular Education curriculum at ninth-grade level
Youth Participation: Iyla has had some minor struggles with being on time to school. Once at school, she completes most of her work without incident. Currently, she has completed 98% of her daily tasks. The uncompleted tasks are those missed during the morning and remain to be made up. As time passes, she is becoming more vocal and her participation is improving.

Pending Meeting Dates: None

Reason for Continued Care: Recent suicidal ideation and self-harm behaviors

Review of Discharge Plan and Estimated Length of Stay: 90 to 120 days, lower level of care such as partial hospitalization or a day treatment program

Treatment Team Attendees: Carla Peterson, M.S., therapist; lyla Jones, youth; Bob and Sarah Jones, parents

Absent Team Members: None

Date of Next Treatment Review: November 27, 20XX, at 10:00 am

cc:

INITIAL TP	Review #1	Review #2	Review #3	Review #4	Review #5	Review #6
dd:						
dt:						

Review #7	Review #8	Review #9	Review #10	Review #11	Review #12	Review #13
dd:						
dt:						

Review #13	Review #14	Review #15	Review #16	Review #17	Review #18	Review #19
dd:						
dt:						

Review #20	Review #21	Review #22	Review #23	Review #24		
dd:						
dt:						

Key Definitions to Remember in Treatment Planning

Accommodation: Slight changes made to the learning environment (setting, timing, response, format, presentation, etc.) that do not impact content learned. Typically included in treatments such as 504 plans; accommodations remove barriers to a youth's ability to learn and to show what they have learned. Some examples include extended time to complete assignments and tests, materials provided in primary language, frequent breaks, proximity seating, reduced distractions, or dividing assignments into smaller, manageable chunks.

Adequate Yearly Progress (AYP): Accountability measures that capture student achievement through various testing modalities. A product of the No Child Left Behind Act of 2001, all students are expected to demonstrate progress toward, and meet at least the minimal requirements of, core content area goals as determined by the state and/or district.

Annual Review: A required yearly meeting in which the team involved in treatment planning and implementation (professionals, caregivers, and other supports) gathers to review and discuss progress toward goals, determine next steps, and make adjustments as needed to ensure maximal gains are made.

Child Find: A mandate of Individuals with Disabilities Education Act (IDEA), this law requires districts to search for and evaluate all youth (early infancy to age 21) suspected of having, or who do have a disability (regardless of degree or severity) that could possibly require special education services.

Due Process: As the guardians of a youth who has specialized services and/or treatment plans, parents/caregivers have certain rights, known as "due process." These rights are one formal approach to resolving any disputes regarding special education (such as disagreements, negligence in following through with treatment plans, etc.).

Extended School Year Services (ESY): Youth receiving special education services may be eligible for supports that extend beyond the normal school year. These supports vary greatly, depending on student needs. ESY eligibility is typically determined during the annual review.

Family Education Rights and Privacy Act (FERPA): A legislation that requires all educational institutions that receive federal funding to protect the privacy of youth. Any identifiable information, such as treatment plans and special services received, must remain private. Access to and release of any of this information is strictly governed.

Free and Appropriate Public Education (FAPE): A mandate of IDEA, all youth have the right to receive education and educational services that meet their individual needs. This includes access to the general curriculum, the opportunity to meet the standards AYP mandated by the state and/or district, and to receive specialized instruction and related services as needed. Educational institutions are required to ensure all youth have FAPE. If for any reason an institution cannot provide FAPE to a youth, they are then required to take necessary steps to ensure that the student's unique needs are met, free of cost to the youth and their family (this could mean adding programs or services within the institution, paying for private school or alternative school tuition, allowing for relocation to a setting that meets specific needs, etc.).

Individuals with Disabilities Education Act (IDEA): Originally written in 1975 and updated in 2004, this legislation ensures all youth receive FAPE and have the opportunity to receive education alongside peers who do not have a disability or disorder.

Individualized Family Service Plan (IFSP): Plans developed in early childhood (sometimes known as infancy and toddler plans) that outline interventions for youth with disabilities and their families. The plans typically involve goals outlined by the team (family, service provider, and a service coordinator) that set the stage for entering the school years.

Informed Consent: A requirement set forth through IDEA, this signed agreement of a parent/caregiver must be obtained before evaluations, revision to plans, or termination of plans can occur.

Interventions: Specific, focused, and purposeful procedures used to support youth who need additional reinforcements in academic, social, emotional, and overall life skills attainment.

Least Restrictive Environment (LRE): Brought forth through IDEA, LRE mandates that educational institutions teach youth with disabilities in a general education setting with appropriate aids and supplements to the maximum extent possible.

Mediation: A step typically taken before due process, mediation is a means for resolving conflict and/or disagreements regarding special education services. The hopes of mediation are that all parties involved can come to an agreement together, rather than having to go through the judicial process.

Modification: Adjustments to the manner, content, extent, and presentation requirements that are used to demonstrate mastery of a concept. Examples could include shortening the length of an assignment, altering the assignment, or changing the way a youth is graded on assignments and projects.

Present Level of Performance (PLOP, PLP): A description of skills, abilities, challenges, and any other pertinent information at the time that a treatment plan is developed. This provides a baseline for creating goals.

Related Services: Any additional developmental or corrective services required for a youth to fully access and benefit from special education. Examples include transportation, speech and language, occupational therapy, or psychological services.

Response to Intervention (RTI): A method for identifying youth who may need additional supports, RTI systematically assesses progress and monitors the effectiveness of supports in place.

Supplementary Aids and Services: Built for use in a general education setting, these aids and services remove barriers that may hinder access to education. Examples include access to assistive technology, large print, modified assignments, or behavioral support.

Triennial Review: A required meeting that takes place every three years in which the team involved in treatment planning and implementation (professionals, caregivers, and other supports) gathers to determine if a youth is still eligible for specialized services and plans.

Q&A: Key Time Frames to Remember in Treatment Planning

(Subject to state mandates. Time frames may vary.)

IEPs

1. **Once a youth is referred, how much time does the school or institution have to schedule an evaluation meeting?**

   The school/institution must schedule an evaluation meeting within a "reasonable amount of time" (usually 10-30 school days).

2. **Once a/any treatment planning meeting has been scheduled, when will parents/caregivers receive written notice of the date/time determined?**

   Most schools/institutions strive to provide written notice of an upcoming meeting within 7-10 calendar days from the chosen meeting time.

3. **How much time is allocated for parents to sign their consent allowing for evaluations?**

   The typical time allocated is 15 school days.

4. **Once the evaluation consent form is signed, how much time does the treatment team have to complete the evaluations and schedule an eligibility meeting?**

   IDEA mandates 60 school days, although some states have shortened this to 30 or 45 school days.

5. **After the meeting, when can parents/caregivers expect to receive all evaluation and paperwork documents?**

   Parents/caregivers can expect these materials to be sent within 3 days of the meeting.

6. **If a parent/caregiver does not agree with the evaluations and therefore requests an Independent Educational Evaluation (IEE), how much time does the team have to respond?**

   The team typically has 30 calendar days to respond to this request.

7. **If eligibility is determined in the initial meeting, when must the team schedule another meeting to create the plan?**

   The team must schedule a planning meeting within 30 calendar days of eligibility determination.

8. **Once developed, when must the plan take effect?**

   The plan must take effect within 30 calendar days of eligibility determination.

9. **How much time does the team have before they must provide copies of the plan to parents/caregivers?**

   Copies of the plan must be sent to parents/caregivers within a "reasonable amount of time" from the plan's creation (usually 10-21 school days).

10. **How often must goals and services be reviewed?**

    Goals and services must be reviewed annually via the Annual Review.

11. **How often must eligibility for treatment plans be reviewed?**

    Eligibility must be reviewed every 3 years via the Triennial Review.

504 Plans

1. **Once a youth is referred, how much time does the school or institution have to schedule an evaluation meeting?**

   The school/institution must schedule an evaluation meeting within a "reasonable amount of time" (usually 10-30 school days).

2. **Once a/any treatment planning meeting has been scheduled, when will parents/caregivers receive written notice of the date/time determined?**

   Most schools/institutions strive to provide written notice of an upcoming meeting within 7-10 calendar days from the chosen meeting time.

3. **What is the time frame given from the initial evaluation meeting to when an eligibility meeting must be scheduled?**

   The team must schedule an eligibility meeting within a "reasonable amount of time" (usually 45-60 calendar days).

4. **What is the time frame given from the eligibility meeting to when a plan development meeting must be scheduled?**

   The team must schedule a plan development meeting within a "reasonable amount of time" (usually 30-45 calendar days).

5. **Once a plan is in place, when should it be expected to take effect?**

   The plan must take effect within a "reasonable amount of time" from the plan's development (usually within 5-7 days).

6. **How often must goals and services be reviewed?**

   Goals and services must be reviewed annually, although parents/caregivers may request to meet before this time.

7. **How often must eligibility for treatment plans be reviewed?**

Eligibility must be reviewed every 3 years.

When the Exceptional Needs of a Youth Are Not Being Met

In very rare cases, certain situations may impede the effectiveness of a treatment plan to the point where the individual needs of a youth cannot be met. This could be due to a lack of resources within an environment, lack of follow through within the team, lack of understanding of needs and ability to reach a youth with profound needs, or any number of reasons. Although very uncommon, extraordinary cases like this do arise. Before exploring avenues to take in this situation, let's take a brief moment to review the key mandates established to protect youth from such failures to provide them with proper support. These mandates can also be found in the "Key Definitions to Remember in Treatment Planning" section of this chapter.

In this scenario, the *Individuals with Disabilities Act* (IDEA) is central to protecting the rights of youth and their families. Among other factors, this legislation ensures that every youth has the right to learn within a *Least Restrictive Environment* (LRE), that parents/caregivers of youth with disabilities are guaranteed procedural safeguards to protect their rights and to ensure their voice is heard when it comes to their child's education, to make certain that *Free and Appropriate Public Education* (FAPE) is provided, and to assure that proper measures are taken when these pieces are not provided. Further, FAPE, a mandate to highlight, ensures that all youth receive, at no cost to families, appropriate accommodations and modifications that meet their individual needs as a youth with a specific disorder or disability. If these rights are not provided, it is time to advocate.

If a treatment provider, caregiver, or team member feels that the current situation, for any reason, does not meet a youth's individual needs, that the current environment is detrimental to success, or that the present situation somehow fails to provide the necessary means for success, they may take action to find solutions in which appropriate supports are put in place. The first step would be to voice concerns with the team and administrative leaders within the present setting. If these concerns go unheard or if actions taken still do not lead to meeting the needs of the youth, the next step would be to negotiate. That includes sharing concerns and coming to an agreement about how to move forward in a way that ensures individual needs are met. If needs are still left unmet, the team would then participate in *mediation*. This may involve having an outside party facilitating the process of determining resolutions. The very last step (which hopefully does not need to be taken) would be *due process*. This formal litigation involves parties proving or disproving the case that a youth is being denied FAPE. The party initiating due process has the burden of proof to demonstrate this potential failure. At its conclusion, the due process ruling must be implemented; however, each party has the opportunity to dispute the ruling. If the ruling involves the purchase of new training, programs, equipment, or even if it involves being transferred to a new setting such as a private school or a specific alternative institution, the parents/caregivers are not responsible for any costs.

Summary

The sample treatment plans in this chapter provide a general glimpse of what one may encounter in various settings. Treatment plan formats may change from institution to institution, state to state, and district to district. Still, the overall purpose, players, and legal mandates remain relatively similar. Just as formatting may shift a bit depending on setting, the definitions and time frames may slightly vary as well but will generally remain similar from state to state and institution to institution. Treatment planners must be aware of mandated time frames, information to include, and stakeholders authorized to be involved in the planning process, and they must ensure that parents/caregivers are aware of these mandates, as well.

>>> QUICK RECAP

Treatment Planning for Youth with Mental Health Disorders:

➤ Treatment plans are a key component in ensuring the successful treatment of symptoms and behaviors involved in mental health disorders.

➤ Treatment planning involves the coming together of various stakeholders (some mandated to attend meetings) in order to create measurable and actionable steps to meet individual needs.

➤ The finalized plan should be considered a "living document" and used to guide the treatment team in their next steps.

➤ The treatment team should be well-versed on terms, important dates, and key factors involved in creating and implementing treatment plans.

When the Youth's Needs Are Not Met:

➤ Parents/caregivers, treatment providers, or anyone on the team has the right to advocate for the youth if they feel their needs are not being met even with a treatment plan.

➤ The first step would be internal advocacy, followed by negation, mediation, and the last step would be litigation/due process.

➤ In situations involving federally funded institutions, under IDEA, costs accrued to meet the needs of a youth must be taken care of so that the family does not have that burden.

Appendix

Basic Social Skills and Their Steps

Following Instructions
1. Look at the person.
2. Say "Okay."
3. Do what you've been asked right away.
4. Check back.

Accepting "No" for an Answer
1. Look at the person.
2. Say "Okay."
3. Stay calm (avoid arguing or complaining).
4. If you disagree, ask later.

Talking with Others
1. Look at the person.
2. Use a pleasant voice.
3. Ask questions.
4. Avoid Interrupting.

Introducing Yourself

1. Look at the person. Smile.
2. Use a pleasant voice.
3. Offer a greeting. Say "Hi, my name is...."
4. Shake the person's hand (when appropriate).
5. When you leave, say "It was nice to meet you [state the other person's name]."

Accepting Criticism (Feedback) or a Consequence

1. Look at the person.
2. Say "Okay."
3. Stay calm (avoid arguing or complaining).

Disagreeing Appropriately

1. Look at the person.
2. Use a pleasant voice.
3. Say "I understand how you feel" or "I hear what you are saying."
4. Respectfully tell why you feel differently.
5. Give a reason.
6. Listen to the other person.

Showing Respect

1. Obey a request to stop a negative behavior.
2. Refrain from teasing, threatening, or making fun of others.
3. Allow others to have their privacy.
4. Obtain permission before using another person's property.
5. Do not damage or vandalize public property.
6. Refrain from conning or persuading others into breaking rules.
7. Avoid acting obnoxiously in public.
8. Dress appropriately when in public.

Showing Sensitivity to Others

1. Express interest and concern for others, especially when they are having troubles.

2. Treat all people with respect, regardless of race, ethnicity, gender, faith, social status, political affiliation, sexual orientation, ability, or differences.

3. Apologize or make amends for hurting someone's feelings or causing harm.

Steps to the Boys Town social skills listed in Chapter 5 can be found in *Teaching Social Skills to Youth, 4th Ed.,* Jeff Tierney and Erin Green, copyright © 2022, Father Flanagan's Boys' Home, Boys Town, NE: Boys Town Press.

References

Achenbach, T.M., & Rescorla, L.A. (2001). **Manual for ASEBA school-age forms & profiles.** Burlington, VT: University of Vermont, Research Center for Children, Youth, and Families.

American Psychological Association (2013). **Diagnostic and statistical manual of mental health disorders,** (2nd ed.). Arlington, VA: Author.

American Psychiatric Association (1994). **Diagnostic and statistical manual of mental disorders,** (4th ed.). Washington, DC: Author.

American Psychiatric Association (1994). **Diagnostic and statistical manual of mental disorders,** (4th ed., text revision). Washington, DC: Author.

Andrade, B.F., Browne, D.T., & Tannock, R. (2014). Prosocial skills may be necessary for better peer functioning in children with symptoms of disruptive behavior disorders. **PeerJ, 2,** e487. https://doi.org/10.7717/peerj.487

Angold, A., Prendergast, M., Cox, A., Harrington, R., Simonoff, E., & Rutter, M. (1995). The child and adolescent psychiatric assessment (CAPA). **Psychological Medicine, 25** (4), 739-753.

Bellini, S. (2006). **Building social relationships: A systematic approach to teaching social interaction skills to children and adolescents with autism spectrum disorders and other social difficulties.** Shawnee Mission, KS: Autism Asperger Publishing Co.

Boys Town National Research Institute for Child and Family Studies. (2006a, April). **Boys Town residential data summary** (Tech, Rep. No. 011-06). Boys Town, NE: Author.

Boys Town National Research Institute for Child and Family Studies. (2006b). **Lasting results: Five-year follow-up study** [Brochure]. Boys Town, NE: Author.

Bronfenbrenner, U. (1979). **The ecology of human development.** Cambridge, MA: Harvard University Press.

Bronfenbrenner, U., & Ceci, S.J. (1994). Nature-nurture reconceptualized in developmental perspective: A bioecological model. **Psychological Review, 101** (4), 568-586.

Centers for Disease Control and Prevention. (2021, March). **Key findings: Children's mental health report.** Retrieved September 21, 2021, from https://www.cdc.gov/childrensmentalhealth/features/kf-childrens-mental-health-report.html

Conners, C.K. (2008). **Conners' comprehensive behavior rating scales manual.** Toronto, ON: Multi-Health Systems, Inc.

Deighton, J., Lereya, S.T., & Wolpert, M. (2021). Enduring mental health in childhood and adolescence: Learning from the millennium cohort study. **Journal of the American Academy of Child & Adolescent Psychiatry, 60** (80), 1030-1039. https://doi.org/10.1016/j.jaac.2020.11.012

Durlak, J.A., Weissberg, R.P., Dymnicki, A.B., Taylor, R.D., & Schellinger, K.B. (2011). The impact of enhancing students' social and emotional learning: a meta-analysis of school-based universal interventions. **Child Development, 82** (1), 405–432. https://doi.org/10.1111/j.1467-8624.2010.01564.x

Egger, H.L., & Angold, A. (2004). The preschool age psychiatric assessment (PAPA): A structured parent interview for diagnosing psychiatric disorders in preschool children. In R. DelCarmen-Wiggins & A. Carter (Eds.), **Handbook of infant, toddler, and preschool mental health assessment** (pp. 223–243). London: Oxford University Press.

Erikson, E.H. (1963). **Youth: Change and challenge.** New York: Basic Books.

Fixsen, D.L., Blasé, K.A., Timbers, G.D., & Wolf, M.M. (2001). In search of program implementation: 792 replications of the Teaching Family Model. In G.A. Bernfeld, D.P. Farrington, & A.W. Leschied (Eds.), **Offender rehabilitation in practice: Implementing and evaluating effective programs** (pp. 149-166). New York: John Wiley & Sons Ltd.

Garcia-Winner, M., & Crooke, P. (2019, September). **The updated and expanded social-thinking competency model: Exploring sensory processing, anxiety management and screen time overload!** Retrieved September 19, 2021, from https://www.socialthinking.com/Articles?name=social-competency-model-attend-interpretproblem-solve-respond

Goldstein, S., & DeVries, M. (2017). **Handbook of DSM-5 disorders in children and adolescents,** (1st ed.). New York: Springer International Publishing.

Gresham, F.M. (1998). Social skills training: Should we raze, remodel, or rebuild? **Behavioral Disorders, 24** (1), 19-25.

Guterman, J.T. (2017, February). **Limitations of the diagnostic and statistical manual of mental health disorders – also known as the DSM-5.** Retrieved from https://jeffreyguterman.medium.com/limitations-of-thediagnostic-and-statistical-manual-of-mental-disorders-alsoknown-as-the-dsm-f864149da182

Handwerk, M.L., Smith, G.L., Thompson, R., Chmelka, M.B., Howard, B.K., & Daly, D.L. (2008). Psychotropic medication utilization at a group home residential care facility. In C. Newman, C.J. Liberton, K. Kutash, & R.M. Friedman (Eds.), **Proceedings of the 20th Annual Florida Mental Health Institute Research Conference. A system of care for children's mental health: Expanding the research base** (pp. 297-300). Tampa: University of South Florida.

Hays, P.A. (2008). **Addressing cultural complexities in practice: Assessment, diagnosis, and therapy,** (2nd ed.). Washington, DC: American Psychological Association.

Huber, L., Plötner, M., & Schmitz, J. (2019). Social competence and psychopathology in early childhood: a systematic review. **European Child & Adolescent Psychiatry, 28** (4), 443-459.

Huefner, J.C., Ringle, J.L., Chmelka, M.B., & Ingram, S.D. (2007). Breaking the cycle of intergenerational abuse: The long-term impact of a residential care program. **Child Abuse & Neglect, 31,** 187-199.

Kingsley, D., Ringle, J.L., Thompson, R.W., Chmelka, B., & Ingram, S. (2008). Cox proportional hazards regression analysis as a modeling technique for informing program improvement: Predicting recidivism in a Boys Town five-year follow-up study. **The Journal of Behavior Analysis of Offender and Victim Treatment and Prevention, 1,** 82-97.

Kohlberg, L. (1981). **The philosophy of moral development: Moral stages and the idea of justice.** New York: Harper and Row.

Larzelere, R.E., Daly, D.L., Davis, J.L., Chemelka, M.B., & Handwerk, M.L. (2004). Outcome evaluation of Boys Town's family home program. **Education and Treatment of Children, 27** (2), 130-149.

Marcia, J.E., Waterman, A.S., Matteson, D.R., Archer, S.L., & Orlofsky, J.L. (1993). **Ego identity: A handbook for psychosocial research.** New York: Springer.

Maryland Advisory Committee to the U.S. Commission on Civil Rights (2019, October). **Disparities in school discipline in Maryland.** Retrieved from https://www.usccr.gov/files/pubs/2020/01-14-MD-SAC-School-Discipline-Report.pdf

Mash, E.J., & Barkley, R.A. (2007). **Assessment of childhood disorders,** (4th ed.). New York: The Guildford Press.

McConaughy, S.H., & Skiba, R.J. (1993). Comorbidity of externalizing and internalizing problems. **School Psychology Review, 22** (3), 421. https://doi.org/10.1080/02796015.1993.12085664

Mental Health Foundation (n.d.). **Learning disabilities.** Retrieved June 4, 2021, from https://www.mentalhealth.org.uk/cy/node/1955

Moses T. (2009). Self-labeling and its effects among adolescents diagnosed with mental disorders. **Social Science & Medicine, 68** (3), 570–578.

National Association of School Psychologists. (2017, December). **Social skills: Promoting positive behavior, academic success, and school safety.** Retrieved from http://www.naspcenter.org/factsheets/socialskills_fs.html

National Association of Special Education Teachers. (n.d.). **Introduction to learning disabilities.** Retrieved June 4, 2021, from https://www.naset.org/index.php?id=2522

National PTA. (2019, February 8). **What is transformative family engagement?** [Video]. YouTube. https://youtu.be/yea1dLDdeK0

Ozbay, F., Johnson, D.C., Dimoulas, E., Morgan, C.A., Charney, D., & Southwick, S. (2007). Social support and resilience to stress: From neurobiology to clinical practice. **Psychiatry (Edgmont), 4** (5) 35-40.

Papalia, D.E., Olds, S.W., & Feldman, R.D. (2005). **A child's world: Infancy through adolescence.** New York: McGraw-Hill.

Payton, J., Weissberg, R.P., Durlak, J.A., Dymnicki, A.B., Taylor, R.D., Schellinger, K.B., & Pachan, M. (2008). **The positive impact of social and emotional learning for kindergarten to eighth-grade students: Findings from three scientific reviews.** Chicago, IL: Collaborative for Academic, Social, and Emotional Learning.

Peter, V.J. (1999). **What makes Boys Town successful.** Boys Town, NE: Boys Town Press.

Piaget, J. (1952). **The origins of intelligence in children.** New York: International Universities Press.

Ratcliffe, B., Wong, M., Dossetor, D., & Hayes, S. (2015). The association between social skills and mental health in school-aged children with autism spectrum disorder, with and without intellectual disability. **Journal of Autism and Developmental Disorders, 45** (8), 2487–2496.

Reynolds, C.R., & Kamphaus, R.W. (2015). **BASC-3: Behavior assessment for children,** (3rd ed.). Bloomington, MN: Pearson.

Ringle, J.L., Chmelka, B., Ingram, S., & Huefner, J. (2006, February) **The sixteen-year post-discharge Boys Town study: Positive outcomes for behaviorally and emotionally troubled youth.** Poster presented at the Midwest Symposium for Leadership in Behavior Disorders, Kansas City, MO.

Risley, T.R. (2005). Montrose M. Wolf (1935-2004). **Journal of Applied Behavior Analysis, 38** (2), 279-287.

Roid, G.H. (2003). **Stanford Binet Intelligence Scales** (5th ed.). Itasca, IL: Riverside Publishing.

Rubin, K.H., Dwyer, K.M., Booth-LaForce, C., Kim, A.H., Burgess, K.B., & Rose-Krasnor, L. (2004). Attachment, friendship, and psychosocial functioning in early adolescence. **The Journal of Early Adolescence, 24** (4), 326-356.

Schaefer, J.D., Caspi, A., Belsky, D.W., Harrington, H., Houts, R., Horwood, L. J., Hussong, A., Ramrakha, S., Poulton, R., & Moffitt, T. E. (2017). Enduring mental health: Prevalence and prediction. **Journal of Abnormal Psychology, 126** (2), 212-224.

Schrank, F.A., McGrew, K.S., & Mather, N. (2014). **Woodcock-Johnson tests of cognitive abilities,** (4th ed.). Rolling Meadows, IL: Riverside Publishing.

Semrud-Clikeman, M. (2007). **Social competence in children.** New York, NY: Springer.

Shaffer, D., Fisher, P., Lucas, C.P., Dulcan, M.K., & Schwab-Stone, M.E. (2000). NIMH diagnostic interview schedule for children version IV (NIMH DISC-IV): Description, differences from previous versions, and reliability of some common diagnoses. **Journal of the American Academy of Child and Adolescent Psychiatry, 39** (1), 28-38.

Spitzberg, B. H. (2003). Methods of interpersonal skills assessment. In J.O. Greene, & B.R. Burleson (Eds.), **Handbook of communication and social interaction skills** (pp. 93-134). Mahwah, NJ: Lawrence Erlbaum Associates Publishers.

Thompson, R.W., Ringle, J.L., & Kingsley, D. (2007, November). **Applying Cox Regression to evaluation of post-treatment studies of the teaching family model.** Paper presented at the Teaching-Family Association 30th Annual Conference, Washington, D.C.

Thompson, R.W., Smith, G.L., Osgood, D.W., Dowd, T.P., Friman, P.C., & Daly, D.L. (1996). Residential care: A study of short- and long-term educational effects. **Children and Youth Services Review, 18,** 221-242.

Tierney, J., & Green, E. (2022). **Teaching social skills to youth: An easy-to-follow guide to teaching 196 basic to complex life skills,** (4th ed.). Boys Town, NE: Boys Town Press.

US Department of Health and Human Services, Center for Behavioral Health Statistics and Quality, Substance Abuse and Mental Health Services Administration (2016). DSM-5 changes: Implications for child serious emotional disturbance. **CBHSQ Methodology Report.** Rockville, MD: Author.

US Department of Health and Human Services, US Department of Education, & US Department of Justice (2000). **Report of the Surgeon General's Conference on Children's Mental Health: A National Action Agenda.** Washington, DC: US Department of Health and Human Services.

Wakefield, J.C. (2016). Diagnostic issues and controversies in DSM-5: Return of the false positives problem. **Annual Review of Clinical Psychology, 12,** 105-132.

Walker-Barnes, C.J., & Mason, C.A. (2001). Ethnic differences in the effect of parenting on gang involvement and gang delinquency: A longitudinal, hierarchical linear modeling perspective. **Child Development, 72,** 1814-1831.

Washington Office of Superintendent of Public Instruction (2021). **Washington state interactive report card.** Retrieved from https://washingtonstatereportcard.ospi.k12.wa.us/ReportCard ViewSchoolOrDistrict/103300

Wechsler, D. (2008). **Wechsler adult intelligence scale,** (4th ed.). San Antonio, TX: Psychological Corporation.

Wechsler, D. (2011). **Wechsler abbreviated scale of intelligence,** (2nd ed.). San Antonio, TX: The Psychological Corporation.

Wechsler, D. (2012). **Wechsler preschool and primary scale of intelligence,** (4th ed.). San Antonio, TX: Psychological Corporation.

Wechsler, D. (2020). **Wechsler individual achievement test** (4th ed.). San Antonio, TX: Psychological Corporation.

Wechsler, D. (2014). **Wechsler intelligence scale for children,** (5th ed.). San Antonio, TX: Psychological Corporation.

Whitney, D.G., & Peterson, M.D. (2019). US national and state-level prevalence of mental health disorders and disparities of mental health care use in children. **JAMA Pediatrics, 173** (4), 389-391.

Wilkinson, G.S., & Robertson, G.L. (2017). **Wide range achievement test,** (5th ed.). Lutz, FL: PAR Psychological Assessment.

Wolf, M.M., Kirigin, K.A., Fixsen, D.L., Blasé, K.A., & Braukmann, C.J. (1995). The teaching-family model: A case study in data-based program development and refinement (and dragon wrestling). **Journal of Organizational Behavior Management, 15** (1/2), 11-68.

Woodcock, R.W., McGrew, K.S., & Mather, N. (2001). **Woodcock-Johnson tests of achievement,** (3rd ed.). Itasca, IL: Riverside Publishing.

Wright, P., & Wright, P. (2008, March). **Key differences between section 504, the ADA, and the IDEA.** Retrieved June 2016 from http://www.wrightslaw.com/info/sec504.summ.rights.htm

Young, G. (2013). Breaking bad: DSM-5 description, criticisms, and recommendations. **Psychological Injury and Law, 6** (4), 345-348.

Index